Ting Tang Tommy

Ting Tang Tommy

88 All-Time Great Games

Simon Godwin

FOURTH ESTATE · *London*

First published in Great Britain in 2009 by
Fourth Estate
An imprint of HarperCollins*Publishers*
77–85 Fulham Palace Road
London W6 8JB
www.4thestate.co.uk

Visit our authors' blog: www.fifthestate.co.uk

1

Quotation from A. A. Milne's *Not That It Matters* reproduced by permission
of Curtis Brown. Quotation from Norman Douglas' *London Street Games*
reproduced by permission of The Society of Authors as the Literary Representative
of the Estate of Norman Douglas. Quotation from Noël Coward's *Hay Fever*
reproduced by permission of A&C Black Publishers and Alan Brodie Representation.

A catalogue record for this book is available from the British Library

ISBN 978-0-00-730957-3

Typeset in Futura Book
Printed in Great Britain by Clays Ltd, St Ives plc

Mixed Sources
Product group from well-managed
forests and other controlled sources
www.fsc.org Cert no. SW-COC-1806
© 1996 Forest Stewardship Council
FSC

For Mum and Dad

Contents

'Why', said the Dodo, 'the best way
to explain it is to do it.'
Lewis Carroll

Introduction

Good games are like good jokes: they get remembered and passed on from person to person. But sometimes they get forgotten. This book is about remembering the best games we've ever known. Games are good for our souls. They are magic recipes for cooking up a good time. Once you know the rules you can bring any situation to life. People crave contact. People crave jollity. People crave games.

This book sets out to prove that you can play games anywhere – on the beach, having dinner with friends, at a barbecue, with your family at Christmas. It's designed to equip you with loads of simple, memorable games that you can share at any moment of the day.

The Games Renaissance starts here.

Games and Me

I've been obsessed with games since I was ten, when I started a club with other kids living nearby. Our club was about one thing only: playing games. We had go-kart races, water fights and football matches that lasted long into the night. We built rafts that we sailed down the local river, sold junk on the street and played wide games in the local park, which was a grassed-over quarry with steep sides called the Brickie. It was a wild time of dusky evenings, confusing crushes and grazed knees. Throughout, being the bossy eldest of four, I got a taste for being in charge and a feeling for what makes the best games great.

As a teenager, I wanted to be an actor so, every Saturday morning, I commuted from St Albans to a drama school in Islington where I learnt 'acting' games. These were different from the *Boy's Own* world of the Club. They were less about heroism and dousing your enemy with a water bomb and more about being spontaneous and inventive. These games encouraged creativity and collaboration. After each class I would practically run back to the station, flushed with hope and exhilaration. I was discovering how the theatre was another version of the Club. As a student I discovered the work of Théâtre de Complicité and saw how they used games to create imaginative and breathtaking works of theatre. Games were a force in their own right. After leaving university I became a theatre director and have been researching and playing games ever since.

A few years ago I started to share the games I had learnt with my friends and family. I discovered they were infectious. At the same time I began asking people to teach me gam
es they knew. I slowly began to amass a collection and the result is this book.

My project is simple: to get grown-ups playing games.

Now, more than ever, we are looking for things to do that are active, communal and affordable: camping, ballroom dancing, knitting, home baking, wild swimming and roller discos are all on the up. People are searching for activities that are easy on the environment, big on fun and which have a whiff of nostalgia for a lost golden age. Games answer this need.

Most of the games in this book are short – fifteen, twenty minutes, half an hour. Played with large numbers of people they can take longer, but my aim is to show that games don't need to be an ordeal. They can come from nowhere and can be played spontaneously with minimum preparation.

All the games in the book have been tested and many are prefaced with an account of how I came to know them, as well as things to watch out for when playing them and occasional references to their historical origin. There are hundreds, even thousands, of games in the world. There are many that I've been forced to leave out. The games that have made it into this book are in the Rolls-Royce category; they are games that I have played and that I know really work.

Where Do Games Come From?

Games are deeply lodged in our culture and history. They have always reflected the beliefs, fears and hopes of an age. Knucklebones grew out of the fortune-teller's bag of tricks and hopscotch is a distant relation of forgotten legends describing labyrinths and mazes. The earliest record we have of game playing

can be found in the ancient palace of Medinet Haboo, at Thebes, in Upper Egypt. Here there is a wall painting showing Rameses III playing a board game with the goddess Isis, wife of Osiris, Lord of the Dead.

The word for play itself has enjoyed a variety of meanings across different cultures. Plato believed that the origin of play lay in the need of all young creatures to 'leap'. *Kridati* is a Sanskrit word that means the play of animals, children and adults, but also refers to the movement of the wind or the waves. Our word for play comes from the Anglo-Saxon *plega*, which means to move fast, to grasp  another's hands, to clap and to play an instrument. The Indo-European root of game, *ghem*, means to 'leap joyfully, to spring' and was used originally to describe the movement of animals as well as people.

Ghem morphed as it was filtered through different European languages. In Old French it became *jambe* and in Italian it became *gamba*. Gradually, words developed that referred to people having fun in groups, such as *jamboree* and *camp* and *campus*. In German the word became *gaman*, in Hellenic it became *kampe* and in Old Norse it became *gems*, which meant 'to come together and congregate as whales do'.

There is something ancient here conveying a sense of people coming together to generate a tribal happiness. This book reflects these visceral origins of playing by including games that are fast, furious and physical. The outdoor games in Chapter 3 revel in ancient ideas of the hunter and the hunted and the power and thrill of running in the landscape. Playing them today gives you a feeling of being part of a tradition that stretches back thousands of years. In Chapter 6 I describe games that have traditionally been played at particular times of the year. These games also stretch back centuries and combine fun with traces of lost rituals.

Many of the games in this book, however, were first written and collected into anthologies by the Victorians. Although many of these had been played for centuries, the Victorians were the first to make an industry out of them. They developed and invented a huge quantity of new games. During the nineteenth century a vast number of games books were published and games became a national obsession.

Why Was This?

Throughout the nineteenth century in Great Britain there was a mass migration to cities. Between 1841 and 1891 the population of London increased from two million to nearly four and a half million. In Scotland there was a comparable surge in Glasgow. The rise in industry and the increase in urban growth led to the formation of a new middle class. These people had left the old, established practices of rural areas to live and work in the city. The days of fairs, bullock running, pigeon flying, cock fighting and village wakes were over. These new communities needed new ways of having fun. They needed games.

And during the same century the new middle class fought for their rights. They achieved shorter working hours, longer holidays and better pay. These innovations, combined with better transport and communication links, freed up time for people to have fun. In the northern cities men joined brass bands; choral singing caught on in the Welsh valleys and pantomimes and music halls started to grip the public imagination. Whist drives, reading groups, picnics, circuses, billiard halls and working men's clubs gained popularity as a new kind of organized fun took hold.

As well as going out and taking part in group activities, people wanted to make their own fun at home. And this appetite was fed by a radical change that was happening inside people's homes: the birth of gas lighting. In our bright, modern homes it's hard for us to imagine what life would have been like by candlelight. If you try counting the lights in the room where you are reading this, I estimate that you will find at least four or five, not including the ambient light that pours in through and around your curtains. At the beginning of the nineteenth century homes were still lit by candles, which were both expensive and of limited strength. Samuel Pepys had to give up writing his diary at only thirty-six because he was worried about going blind – 'and so to bed, being weary, sleepy, and my eyes begin to fail me, looking so long by candlelight upon white paper' – he wrote in 1663. In the centuries of darkness games were things to be played outdoors while inside people told stories, sang songs and played instruments. Pleasure came from the things you imagined rather than saw.

The social historian Dorothy Flanders gives a detailed account of the development of domestic gas lighting in her book *The Victorian House*. She explains how Friedrich Albert Winsor became one of the first popular exponents of gas lighting in the home, through a series of public lectures and brochures. In 1814 Winsor founded a company with a single gasometer. By 1852 there were forty-seven gasometers in Britain and a network of gas piping, stretching over two hundred miles. The craze for gas lighting spread fast. By 1816 gas was common in London and by 1823 fifty-three cities had gas companies. By the middle of the century, it had become a presence in most small towns and even in some villages. The contemporary journalist G. A. Sala provides a vivid insight into the difference it made to everyday life:

> In broad long streets where the vista of lamps stretches far away into almost endless perspective; in courts and alleys, dark by day but lighted up by this incorruptible tell-tale; on the bridges; in the deserted parks; on wharfs and quays; in dreary suburban roads; in the halls of public buildings; in the windows of late-hour-keeping houses and offices, there is my gas – bright, silent, secret. Gas to teach me; gas to counsel me; gas to guide my footsteps.

As well as illuminating streets, gas changed how rooms were lit. The Argand Lamp became a popular innovation in middle-class homes. In stark contrast to the uneven light of candles, the Argand Lamp burned gas at a higher temperature, which created a purer flame. This new, brighter flame was also contained for the first time in a glass cylinder, which saved it from draughts and allowed the flame to be raised or lowered, rather like the modern dimmer switch. Brightness could now be controlled and modulated at will. It was also possible for gas to be run through pipes and tubes to special fittings in the ceilings and walls, even to tables. Wall sockets had flexible attachment points so that lights could be directed towards particular people or objects. The arrival of gas lighting meant that everyone – not just the rich – could now play games long into the night.

And so, for the Victorians, the stage was set for a games revolution to take hold. Is it time for us to discover once again the easy pleasure and communal happiness that only games can offer?

The Original and Best Games for a Party

I want to show you how games can be played anywhere. But parties are the place where most of us get our first taste, so let's start there. When I say party I am thinking of a group of adults or a family gathering with a good spread of ages. There have been lots of books on children's party games so that's not my remit here. I want to share forgotten but universal games that can be played by all.

At a party, timing is important. You have to wait for a lull. You have to wait until the group wants something new. And not everyone may want to play. This is fine. You are looking for a majority. If you can get most people onboard, a game is possible. Never force people to play. They can either just watch or you can give them special roles – like being the referee, timer or scorer. Everyone likes to feel included.

Arriving

Games that welcome people are fun. You might have a large jar of sweets near the door and get people to write down what they think is the correct number on a sheet of paper nearby. It's nice to have something to announce later in the evening and even nicer for the person who gets to walk away with the jar of sweets. Another good ice-breaker is to ask everyone to bring a photograph of themselves as babies. As people are helping themselves to a glass of wine, you can fix each photograph to a piece of cardboard with a number under each one. On pieces of paper against the numbers, people can write down who they think is who. It's a great moment at midnight, or towards the end of the night, to bring in the photo board and to ask each grown-up baby to step forward one by one. You can award a prize to the winner but the fun comes from seeing how the babies in the photographs express the intangible essence of the grown-ups they become, something which never quite leaves them.

Mister Hit

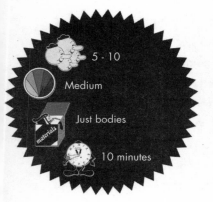

5 - 10

Medium

Just bodies

10 minutes

This game was taught to me by a teacher of clowning in Paris. It's amazingly good fun and is a great test of coordination. It's also very good to play as one of your first games because it gets everyone on their feet and is a brilliant way to learn everyone's names. As the host of the party, you might know who everyone is but most probably your guests won't. This is one of those classic games that takes a minute to learn and a lifetime to master.

Everyone stands in a circle. Someone is nominated as Mister Hit. Their job is to tap the person standing to their left or right, preferably on the shoulder. The person tapped must say someone else's name in the circle. This person then becomes Mister Hit and must, in turn, tap someone else to their left or right. So the basics are: when you are hit you call someone's name and when your name is called you hit someone.

After a few practice rounds the game becomes fun as you explain that there will now be no hesitation between hitting and speaking. There must be an unbroken chain of hits and names. Don't be afraid to be harsh. As soon as someone hesitates, or speaks when they should hit or hits when they should speak, they are eliminated.

You carry on playing until three remain for a Mister Hit final, after which the two last players are declared the winners.

Lie Detector

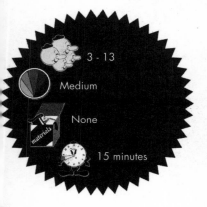

3 - 13

Medium

None

15 minutes

This is also not strictly a party game but an ice-breaker. I sometimes use it on the first day of rehearsals to get people talking about themselves in a playful way. It encourages the rest of the group to work together to interrogate the person on the spot. It needs to be played with a group of people who don't know each other that well so that no one enjoys a particular advantage.

Each player shares three things about themselves. Two of these must be true. One must be false. In the spirit of Radio Four's *The Moral Maze*, everyone in the group is given the chance to interrogate the speaker. The group grills the speaker to discover how well they can back up their claims. You can limit the number of questions each person is allowed to ask if the group is big. When everyone has had the chance to ask their questions, the group decides together which statement they believe to be the false one. This is the most fun part as everyone struggles to reach a consensus. When a majority decision has been reached, you announce your verdict and discover whether you've successfully deciphered fact from fiction. Watch out for hesitation, faintly concealed smiles and discreet blushing.

Blind Man's Buff

5 - 25

Easy

Blindfold, two spoons

10 minutes

In the ancient Egyptian tombs of Beni Hassan there is a mural showing a man kneeling with his head down and others standing behind him with clenched fists raised above his back. It has been suggested that these men are playing Hot Cockles, or 'Who Struck?' as the game was also known.

Hot Cockles is a violent game with a rich tradition. It belonged to what the Greeks called the kolla bismos *family of games: 'buffeting' games. A player is blindfolded and then struck by each player in turn. The blindfolded player had to guess the identity of his assailants by the quality of their slap.*

The game also contained the potential for romance. It seems that the fun lay in decoding the hidden suggestions within the blow. In a Christmas edition of the Spectator from 1711, a joke correspondent wrote: 'I am a Footman in a great family and am in love with the House Maid. We were all at Hot Cockles last night in the Hall; when I lay down and was blinded, she pulled off her shoe and hit me with the Head such a Rap, as almost broke My Head to Pieces. Pray, Sir, was this Love or Spite?'

Alongside Hot Cockles there developed the variation we all know, Blind Man's Buff. This game proved too rowdy for Samuel Pepys. On 26 December 1664 he wrote in his diary, 'I to bed, leaving them to their sport and Blind Man's Buff.' We later discover that the party continued until 4.00 a.m.

Today there are loads of variations but the version I prefer is a silent one. Any game that encourages the gentle crossing of boundaries is supercharged with fun and danger. Just taking out a blindfold can cause minor hysteria and as soon as an element of touch is introduced people go crazy, especially after a few drinks.

A brave individual is blindfolded. Everyone else takes up their positions – in corners, on chairs, lying on the floor, wherever feels most fun. They must remain there without making a sound. The blindfolded player must identify each player only by touch. As chuckling or giggling gives the game away immediately, it's very important that everyone keeps silent. The game lasts either until everyone is correctly identified or you can switch after the first person is identified, that person then taking over the blindfold.

A wacky variation is to arm the blindfolded player with two spoons. He then uses these in place of hands. You can just about make out height, hair length, size of nose, breasts or not etc. Here avoiding laughter is impossible: the feeling of two cold spoons being passed over your face and other parts is quite overwhelming.

General Post

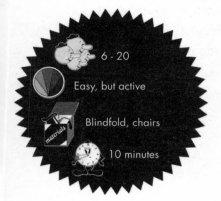

6 - 20

Easy, but active

Blindfold, chairs

10 minutes

The Penny Post was started on 10 January 1840 and Sir Rowland Hill was the first Postmaster General. Throughout the nineteenth century steamships and trains revolutionized the train service, so it's no surprise that a game arose reflecting the impact of these dramatic changes. Playing the game today, there is something pleasurably antique about it. It's also surprisingly lively, gets the blood flowing and allows you to use your blindfold once again.

Everyone sits on chairs in a large circle. Someone is appointed Postmaster while everyone else chooses cities in the world. These cities are destinations for the post and the Postmaster must remember them all. It will be his job to call out the origins and destinations of the mail. At the start, one player is blindfolded and placed in the middle of the circle. The game begins when the Postmaster calls out the first journey using the cities around the circle. He might say, 'The post is going from Berlin to New York'. And so now the person who is Berlin must change places with the person who is New York. They must do this without the blindfolded player either touching them or getting to an empty chair before they do. The player who is touched, or whose chair is taken, must take over the blindfold. To get everyone moving, the Postmaster can occasionally call 'General Post', which means that all the players have to change seats, giving the blindfolded player an excellent chance to grab someone or a seat. Play until everyone who wants to has had a go in the middle.

Caterpillar

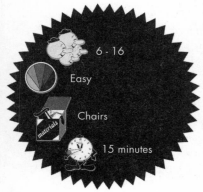

6 - 16

Easy

Chairs

15 minutes

This is a more urgent version of General Post, played without the blindfold. It's used a lot by theatre directors to create a 'group mind'. It encourages everyone to work together and it's fantastic when the whole group is working as one. It's both fast and physical.

Begin by making a circle of chairs. Everyone sits down apart from one person who remains standing in the centre. His or her chair remains empty. The game revolves around this player's attempt to sit down on an empty chair while the other players work to stop them. To do this players have continually to move from one chair to another. As soon as one chair has been vacated another bottom must fill it. Players can move from side to side and across the circle. As soon as the centre player manages to occupy a seat, the dislodged player takes over.

Psychiatrist

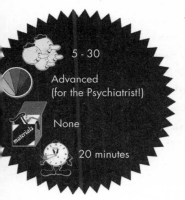

5 - 30

Advanced
(for the Psychiatrist!)

None

20 minutes

This is a game that, in the nineteenth century, would have been called a 'catch' game because you are looking to catch someone out. You can only play the game if someone in the group doesn't know the secret and is willing to be a good sport. It's pretty difficult and I've never known anyone to solve it without plenty of clues. It works best if all your players are aged ten upwards.

A Psychiatrist is selected from the group. It's his job to diagnose the condition everyone is suffering from. He leaves the room while the group agrees what condition they might all have. There are unlimited options but the classic ruse is that everyone answers as if they are the person sitting to their left. The Psychiatrist returns to the room and starts to ask questions of his or her patients. How are they? What do they like doing? Do they have any particular fears, dreams etc? People have to answer as accurately as possible according to their knowledge of the person to their left (which itself proves very revealing). When the Psychiatrist is completely baffled you can help him by suggesting he ask each patient their name.

The Scissors Game

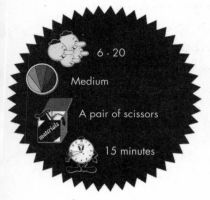

6 - 20

Medium

A pair of scissors

15 minutes

This is another 'catch' game. I am always the last to catch on to the 'key' of these games, so I am very happy to pass on the secret to this one. If you are ever asked to play it, you will now be one of those in the know.

This game works best with plenty of people. Everyone sits in a circle, and only a small number (ideally no more than two) should know the rules of the game. A pair of scissors is passed around and around the circle. Each time you pass it to the person next to you, you have to say 'I PASS THE SCISSORS CROSSED' or 'I PASS THE SCISSORS UNCROSSED'. The recipient has to say 'I RECEIVE THE SCISSORS CROSSED' or 'I RECEIVE THE SCISSORS UNCROSSED'. The people who don't know the rules will begin by assuming that the words relate to the state of the scissors and whether the blades are open or not, and the people who know the rules can take advantage of this. Actually, each statement refers to whether the players who are passing and receiving the scissors have their LEGS crossed or uncrossed. As you go around the circle, as people make statements that are false they lose a life. Three lives lost and they're out. People become more and more frustrated but eventually they begin to cotton on to the rules and subtly try and keep the people who don't understand from working them out. When all the players left in the circle get it, the game is over and everyone can have another drink.

Word Tennis

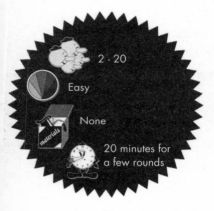

2 - 20

Easy

None

20 minutes for
a few rounds

Every Friday during my teenage years I would catch the train from St Albans to King's Cross and walk up Pentonville Road to the Anna Scher Theatre School. I was obsessed with acting and had decided that this was to be my path into show business. The walls of the foyer were covered with photographs of famous pupils, past and present. Most of the cast of Grange Hill were up there, alongside stars from EastEnders and actors like Kathy Burke, Jake Wood and Patsy Palmer.

The school was one big studio in which all the classes took place. At the back of the room, on a raised platform, sat three washing baskets filled with props and costumes, a bus stop sign and a small record player. Every week I would enter, pay my pound for the class and sit quietly at one side of the room. There would be little talking, just an atmosphere of silent expectancy as we waited for the arrival of Anna. Everyone would sit, carefully scanning each other.

There were sixty of us in a class. Kids came from all over London but especially from the areas nearby – King's Cross, Islington and Highbury. These were not privileged stage school types, but local working-class kids who loved acting. There was no audition or interview, just a four-year waiting list. When your name came up you would start the following week.

The school was like a boxing club. You went there and for two hours *you improvised the most intense, unflinching scenes you could. Domestic violence, drugs, alcoholism and broken families all featured heavily. For the first six months I was practically silent. I felt nervous and confused. Acting had always been about scripts. Doing a play involved being given a part, learning my lines and then performing on the night. But in this world spontaneity was everything. With your partner you would be given a first line ('That was bang out of order!', 'You do nothing round the house!', 'I've had it up to here with you!') and, in front of everyone, you would have to improvise a situation. There was no time for throat clearing – bang, you were in the scene. And the style was direct, confrontational and fast. The scenes rocketed up the emotional scale as you let rip on your colleague. This training taught me a lot about how to play games. My eight years at Anna's taught me that thinking on your feet and embracing the unexpected is the place where creativity begins.*

Some weeks, if the class had been particularly intense, we would end with a game. The one I enjoyed most was Word Tennis. Since learning the game at Anna's I've played it in many different contexts. It can be played standing up in a line or sitting down and children and grannies love it. It's called Word Tennis because the aim is to keep the word rally going for as long as possible.

Everyone sits in a circle, either on chairs or round a table. Someone starts by suggesting a category with lots of members, for example, Sports. The person gives an example of the category (football) and the game begins. Travelling in a clockwise direction, each person must give an example from that category. If it's Sports, people might say basketball, hockey, or tennis. You keep going until someone hesitates, repeats a name or can't think of another one. After a few trial runs you can start eliminating people. When someone is out you start again with a new category. If you have been playing sitting down, when you get to the last four people still in, ask them to stand up. This increases the stakes. You keep going until only two people are left in. Everyone suggests categories for the final and you have a dramatic showdown.

Fun categories really help. Here are some you might like to try:

Sweets and Chocolates
Things that Live Under the Sea
Types of Footwear
Things People Do to Keep Warm
Things You Might Find in a Convent
Things People Do When They're in Love
Dwellings
Things that Cost Under £1
High-Street Stores
Contents of a Lady's Handbag

Fairytale Characters
Five-Letter Words
Fairground Rides
Three-Letter Words
Precious Stones
Horror Films
Fashion Designers
Sandwich Fillings
Objects with Doors
Politicians

Empire

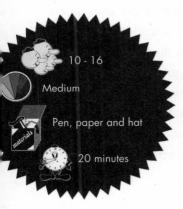

10 - 16

Medium

Pen, paper and hat

20 minutes

Some games have a beautiful form, like this one. Its design is simple but deeply satisfying. Although you might feel it's too simple to last very long it's surprisingly difficult and unravels slowly. It's perfect for a big crowd and tremendously accessible.

Everyone writes the name of a famous person down on a scrap of paper. They then fold up their bits of paper and throw them into a hat. The umpire also writes a name on a piece of paper and adds it to the hat. This name will be known as the Wild Card.

The umpire takes the names out of the hat and reads them aloud to the group twice through, explaining to the group that they must remember as many names as possible. The names are now put back into the hat, which is placed to one side. The umpire then selects a player to start. This player must try and guess which player has written which name. They might start by suggesting that their bookish elder brother is Paul Auster, or their trendy younger sister Vivienne Westwood. If this player guesses correctly then the person whose name they have guessed must join their empire. They may confer with their new recruit to keep remembering names and guessing who wrote them. If they keep guessing correctly, their empire expands accordingly.

If a player guesses wrongly, the turn passes to this player whose name hasn't been guessed. They take over and begin to guess names. If they manage to guess the name of a person who has already accrued an empire, this person and all her captured players move to this new emperor. The game ends when one person has subsumed everyone into one huge domain. The aim is to remember all the names and to match them all accurately to their source.

The first time you play this, you might want to ask every-one just to write down names without telling them what is to come. People will write names that clearly reflect their interests and tastes. They will be easy to guess. You will play the first round and people will be a little non-plussed. Then, having played the game, ask everyone to disguise themselves by writing a name no one would expect. So the young proto-feminist in the group might write Jeremy Clarkson, the bookish elder brother Sporty Spice and the mild-mannered granny Sid Vicious. This time the game takes longer and becomes fascinating as everyone tries to guess who is behind each name. The names act like masks.

Crucial to the game's success is the Wild Card. The status of the Wild Card cannot be established definitively since the umpire who wrote it cannot be questioned. Empires have to establish for themselves which name is the red herring.

The aim of the game is world domination. So what's new?

Cheeky Golf

Unlimited

Advanced
(takes skill in certain areas!)

Fifty pence piece,
pint glass

Variable
(depending on
success)

*When I learnt this game recently at a
party I was pretty alarmed and sceptical;
was it dangerous? Was it too shocking?
Was it even possible? Well, after having
played the game myself I can testify that
it's perfectly safe, deeply strange but very
good fun. It is a game in which partici-
pation should not be made obligatory,
for reasons that will become clear. And
no articles of clothing need be removed.
It was taught to me by a woman wearing
a skirt and I did fine in jeans …*

You need a fifty pence piece and a pint glass. Establish a
line a few metres from the glass and ask a volunteer to
stand behind it. The player then takes the fifty pence piece
and clenches it between his buttocks. Keeping hold of the
coin, the player then attempts to walk forward before
successfully releasing it into the glass. Players can either
drop the coin from a height or try and squat over the
glass. Although the idea may strike the assembled
company as too awful for words, it's actually very
straightforward. Our muscles in this area are strong and
carrying a coin around is actually pretty easy. There is also
the most remarkable joy in hearing the tinkle of the coin

landing in the glass: it's probably the nearest we'll come to the satisfying pleasure of laying an egg.

If you have the appetite to go further, you can think about creating an obstacle course between you and the pint glass, using chairs and other bits of furniture.

The Cereal Game

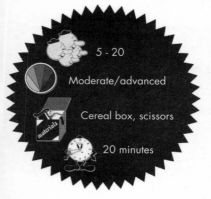

5 - 20

Moderate/advanced

Cereal box, scissors

20 minutes

If you're playing with a big group, it's especially important to find games that sustain people's interest even after they have been eliminated. You need games that are fun for spectators as well as participants. This game fits that bill well. It's fun watching men struggling with it, since it's often women who are more supple and therefore better at it. It can be a bit tough on the neck, so if you have problems in this area, steer clear of the game or make sure you do a few stretches first. People who do lots of yoga invariably do very well.

The aim of this game is to pick up the cereal box using your teeth, with only your feet touching the ground.

Place the cereal box in the centre of the circle, far away from any coffee tables or furniture. Go around the circle, with everyone having a go. Most people will manage to bend over and lift the box into the air using their teeth without too many problems. Next, using a pair of scissors cut off a strip around the top of the box, so that it's something like a fifth lower. Now, go round again, remembering that if any part of the body – apart from the feet – makes contact with the ground the person goes out.

This includes players losing their balance. Keep going for about five rounds, with the packet being cut down lower and lower each time. More and more people will go out until you are left with your finalists. If the remaining individuals are demonstrating a rare expertise, then for your very final round you can cut off the lip of the packet entirely so that players have to suck the horizontal piece of card off the floor while essentially being upside down.

I have seen it done.

Clap Volleyball

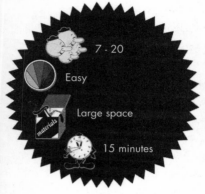

7 - 20

Easy

Large space

15 minutes

When I was at Cambridge I shared a dream with my friend Charles Dean of touring a play around Russia. For both of us it quickly became an obsession. Charles was a producer and his vision was that we would travel the country, performing the show in exchange for food and accommodation. The challenge began to engross him more and more. He persuaded a girl studying Russian to become the tour translator and the project grew in scale. In his small attic room he pinned on the wall a huge map of the former Soviet Union and nearby countries. Red pins would signify a confirmed date. Every time I visited Charles, the red pins would have multiplied and after some months we had dates in Moscow, St Petersburg, Belarus, Estonia, Lithuania, Latvia and Poland.

We had decided to tour The Winter's Tale, with a cast of ten and minimal props. Even with no scenery, transporting cast and equipment became a major headache. Trains were cumbersome and journeys time-consuming. We only had a month during our holidays and Charles was determined that we made all our dates. I was becoming more and more anxious but Charles reassured me that he would find a way and that I should simply concentrate on casting and rehearsing the show.

On the first day of the tour we gathered outside the Maypole pub in Cambridge to find one large coach and two rather confused-looking drivers. The plan was simple. We were to climb aboard and then drive, via Berlin, to Moscow for our first performance. From there we would drive across the former Soviet bloc, criss-crossing countries to deliver our pared-down version of Shakespeare. And so began a remarkable month of eleven overnight journeys, bus drivers being taken to the verge of madness, passionate love affairs, late-night border inspections and unending streams of vodka.

Somehow we made it on time for our first performance in Moscow. The show went well and the cast and I were invited to attend a workshop at the Moscow State University, given by a director and expert in the Stanislavski Method. We expected two hours of rigorous emotional exercises. What we got was a lot of clapping. The director explained how awareness, contact and speed were at the heart of his approach to theatre. And so he taught us this simple but potent game, which I have played in practically every rehearsal room I have been in since. It works with friends, too. You need a big space, but the joy is that, although it's a kind of volleyball, you can play it indoors since there is no ball to break anything with …

You need a minimum of seven players: two teams of three plus one umpire. Begin by asking the teams to choose names, and then get them to stand opposite each other in two lines. Just as in real volleyball, appoint someone on Team A to serve. Their job will be to make clear eye contact with someone on Team B and fire the clap to them. Without hesitation, this player must send the clap back to someone else on Team A and so a rally begins. Teams drop points by indirect clap throwing. Equally, if the clap is clearly aimed at someone but they are dozing and there is a split-second lull, the other team gains a point. The aim is to create fast and furious rallies that last until concentration reaches breaking point.

Smashes are allowed, but they carry risks. Rather than directing the clap straight to the opposite team, players may pass the clap down the line to someone on their own side. However, if this person is distracted and hesitates then the other team wins a point. The clap may be passed along a team as many times as players wish, but everyone must maintain their position in the line and any hesitation must be leaped on and penalized by the umpire. The first team to score five points wins.

When I'm the umpire I build tension by winding up both teams as much as possible to win. When you've appointed a player to serve, tell them to wait for a visual cue. This gives everyone a chance to regain their focus. Position yourself between the lines at one end and begin by crying, 'Let's play Clap Volleyball!'

Mickey Mouse

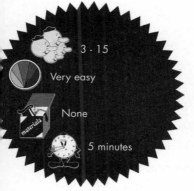

3 - 15

Very easy

None

5 minutes

When I was starting out as a theatre director one of my earliest projects was a collaboration with the poet Simon Armitage. I had been a fan of his work for ages and, after leaving university, I had the idea of trying to persuade him to write a new version of a Greek tragedy called Heracles. Often, Greek tragedies are translated by academics rather than poets and I was convinced Simon could bring a raw, contemporary edge to the language of Euripides. I sent Simon the script of the play and he wrote back saying he would be very interested in doing the job, provided I could guarantee the play would actually get staged. Faced with this Herculean challenge, I began contacting theatres, trying to find a venue that would not only pay for the commission but would give an assurance that, barring natural disaster, they would stage the play. Theatres were excited about Simon Armitage but were less excited about Simon Godwin. Eventually, I persuaded the West Yorkshire Playhouse in Leeds – Simon's local theatre – to meet me. Over the course of an hour I struggled to communicate my passion for the original play and its potential impact if rewritten by Simon.

Touched by my overpowering enthusiasm (if nothing else), the theatre decided to commission the play and so began a two-year process of writing and workshops to develop a new work – Mister Heracles – based on Euripides' original.

The plot of the play was profoundly serious. The drama tells the story *of a triumphant Heracles returning home after the completion of his labours only to suffer a breakdown and murder his wife and children. During rehearsals it was easy to become sucked into the play's darkness and, to keep our spirits up, we played games. In order to work, these needed to be as silly and lively as possible. One of the actors in the cast taught us this game, which fitted the bill perfectly.*

This game doesn't need many players to work. Playing with a small number of people is actually better as you have to be on your toes even more than usual.

Everyone stands in a circle. The player who starts covers his nose with his fist to make a Mickey Mouse nose. The player to his right places his left hand behind his left ear to make a Mickey Mouse ear. The player to the left places his hand behind his right ear to make a Mickey Mouse ear on the other side. So you now have a nose and two ears made by three different players. The player with the nose now throws it across the circle to another player who 'catches' it. That person now has the Mickey Mouse nose and the two players either side of him must make the ears on the correct sides.

The nose is now 'thrown' faster and faster around the circle. You will find that people consistently forget to make the ears at the right time on the right side. Keep going until the nose is constantly moving, with hands moving from ears to noses to ears. The aim is to heighten everyone's awareness of what is happening and to develop fast, intuitive reactions.

You can introduce a competitive edge by eliminating people who make a mistake. Or you can just play for the fun of it – enjoying the swirl of ears and noses. Some years later, I saw one of the actors at a crowded opening night in a theatre in London. Across the crowded stalls he 'threw me a nose'.

Chinese Pictures

5 - 15

Medium

Pens and paper

45 minutes

It's always exciting to spot new games as they hit the scene. No one knows where they come from but suddenly there is a tipping point and everyone is playing them. I was thrilled to discover this game a few months ago. It's already being played by more and more people I know and when you play it you'll understand why. It's a very well structured game and I think it's a 'non-submersible', which means that it can withstand any context or degree of skill. It comes with its own inscribed magic.

This game is a variant on the Consequences model, which I discuss in Chapter 4. The origins of this game are hinted at in a book called Kate Greenaway's Book of Games from 1889. Here one player draws a famous scene from history or fiction and the other players have to write down what they think it is, before folding their suggestion over and passing their paper on. At the end players unfold their papers and read out a list of possible definitions. But this version, where everyone is constantly drawing and writing, is a lot more fun.

Everyone begins with a pile of papers, each about the size of a quarter of a piece of A4. It's crucial that you begin with the right number of papers. For an odd number of players you'll need the same number of papers; for an even number of players you will need one less. So for nine players you'll need nine papers, for eight you'll need seven. On their first piece of paper everyone writes down a film title. Now everyone passes their entire pile, with the title still on top, to the person on their left. This player looks at the title and places it at the bottom of the pile. Now they must attempt to draw the film title on this new piece of paper. They can do this either by breaking down the title of the film or by drawing an image that communicates its essential content. When this is done, players pass the entire pile to the player on their left. This person looks carefully at the picture and then puts it to the bottom of the pile and on the next new piece of paper writes down the title that it suggests to them. When they have done this they pass their entire pile to the person on their left, who reads the title, places it on the bottom and draws the picture that expresses it. It's essential that the entire pile is passed on each time and this process of reading/writing/drawing continues until people get their original title back.

After they have been reunited with their original title, each player now reveals their sequence of words and pictures. Players talk through their sequence, holding up one paper at a time. A potential example might go: I wrote down *One Flew Over the Cuckoo's Nest*, Dad drew [show strange drawing of a flying bird]; Granny wrote *Chicken Run*, Mum drew [an abstract figure distantly related to a chicken fleeing a prison] and Grandpa wrote *The Fugitive*, and so on.

It's fantastically rewarding when one series of papers manages to successfully convey one consistent title, but this is pretty rare. There is no winner; the pleasure lies in the often crazy relationship between image and title. Players should do their best to be as precise and detailed as possible but more often than not this is a celebration of distortion. Also, don't be put off by people being confused or grudging at the start. The game reveals its magic gradually and it's always thrilling to discover the way you arrive back at your title and the mad journeys everyone has gone on.

It's a Knockout in Your Living Room

Playing games with lots of people is not easy. Arriving at a party, people's expectation is to drink a lot and talk. So when someone proposes a game there may be some resistance. There is a failsafe way to short-circuit this and that's by exploiting the human animal's competitive gene. As soon as you put people in a team they are overtaken with a desire to win at all costs. Suddenly, you have people obsessed with potential strategies and ways to prove their skills to their team-mates. Everyone becomes desperate to avoid the humiliation of being the one who lost the match.

You will discover how, once a team has played a game together, they become hungry to stay together to play more. With this in mind, I have put together a series of games here that can be played consecutively. If you are feeling really motivated you can create a score board and build up a championship-type vibe. I'm thinking a 'games decathlon'. You can have an interval halfway through when people can drink and chat before getting going again, with even crazier and more adventurous games.

Slap Penny

Min. 8

Moderate

Twenty pennies, four chairs

10 minutes

This game is good because it's a relatively sedate way to start a run of team games. It takes skill but it's not too complex or too physical. It allows people to start working together and the penny slapping technique is not as easy as it seems.

For this game you'll need two teams with a minimum of four people in each team. The two teams stand facing each other. At either end of each row place a chair (so you'll need four chairs in total). On the two chairs facing each other at one end of the line, place a pile of ten pennies. When the umpire shouts 'Go', the two players on each team standing next to the chairs pick up a coin and place it on their hand. They have to hold their hand and palm upwards, with the penny resting in the palm.

The penny is then slapped from that palm to another and then onto the palm of the next player, who in turn transfers it to his other hand, and so on. The first player palms the coins from the pile as quickly as he can to get as many pennies travelling down the line as possible. The last player in the line drops the coin onto the chair standing beside them.

A penny may never be clutched. If it is dropped, it must be returned to the starting point on the chair. If you really want to test your players, when all ten coins have arrived you can demand that they send them back again. The first team to slap all their coins home wins.

Leaping Cards

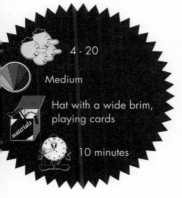

4 - 20

Medium

Hat with a wide brim, playing cards

10 minutes

Playing cards are fiendishly difficult to throw. They are resistant to too much force and their shape means that you have to find an oblique approach to getting them on target. This game was originally played by the Victorians who would try and throw cards into a top hat. Sadly, most of us don't keep one to hand anymore. But you do need a stiff hat with a wide brim. I have an old trilby, for example, that works perfectly well. Alternatively, a pudding basin or small bucket will both work well.

Here I have adapted the original, rather sedate game into a high-octane team competition. The game has acquired a greater urgency as you now have to balance accuracy with speed.

The aim of the game is to be the team that wins as many points as possible. The game ends when one team has managed to throw all their cards.

Begin by spreading a newspaper on the ground and placing your hat in the centre of it. Using a jumper, scarf or the edge of a rug, establish a line around 1.5 metres from the hat. This will be where players throw their cards from.

Divide the company into two teams. Each team is given half a pack of cards. One team has the red cards and the other the black cards. On 'Go', one by one a member of each team goes to the line and throws a card towards the hat. For every card that makes it successfully into the hat, players are awarded three points, for any that land on the rim players get two points and for any card that at least makes it onto the newspaper, players get one point. In the fast and furious snowstorm of cards, leave the scoring until all the cards have been thrown.

Both teams scramble to throw their cards as accurately and as rapidly as possible. When one team has succeeded in throwing all their cards, the game stops. At this point the two team captains begin by collecting all their team's cards that have landed around the room, which are discarded as they are worth no points. They then collect all the cards on the newspaper, which are worth one point. The captains should count as they go, moving on to gather cards on the brim (two points) and then in the hat itself (three points). The team with the highest score wins.

Picture This

6 - 24

Easy

Paper, pens,
display board

15 minutes

*There are various board games that you
can buy in the shops based around
drawing. Pictionary and Articulate are
two good examples that revolve around
a very simple premise. Indeed, the
premise is so simple that you can easily
play your own versions at home, with
stuff you already have. Unlike Chinese
Pictures, this game is competitive and is
played with a time pressure; this means
you can happily include it in your games
tournament.*

*Drawing games are like charades in that they ask for skills that most
people don't have to any great level. This is exactly why they are such
fun.*

You need a pinboard, which you can cover with sheets of
A4 paper, or single sheets of A3, depending on what you
have to hand and the size of your board. After forming
two teams, each player writes three everyday objects on a
different piece of paper and throws those bits of paper into
a hat. The game begins with the first player pulling out a
piece of paper from the hat and drawing the object on the
board, which must be guessed by the rest of her team.
Each player is given only thirty seconds to try and draw as
many objects as possible. As the names are guessed
correctly, the team keeps their papers to add up when the

hat has eventually been cleared. The team with the most names at the end wins.

The Sofa Game

6 - 20

Easy/perilous

Two plastic bottles,
a low, soft sofa

10 minutes

It is with some trepidation that I share this game. It's a game that can end in tears and possibly even injury. It takes the childhood fun of making obstacle courses and gives it a competitive edge. However, only play this game if you have the right sofa. You need one which is low, soft and bouncy. I have one in my flat that is essentially just a piece of foam. For sitting on, it's hell. For this game, it's perfect.

This game is a relay race. To prepare, you'll need two plastic bottles. They can be large mineral water bottles or medium-sized plastic milk bottles. Form two lines. On 'Go', the first player of each team must put the bottle between their knees, climb over the sofa, touch the back wall of the room and clamber back again. If the bottle slips from between their legs, they have to stop and replace it. The returning player tags the next in line and the first team to make it home wins.

You should position the sofa in the middle of the room, some way from the back wall. Inevitably, the sofa will tip over with the weight of two players fighting to scramble over it, so you need plenty of space and a light sofa that isn't going to crush anyone. When I played the game recently it was hilarious seeing a group of people in their early thirties coming up with the most amazingly ingenious solutions to scaling the sofa while maintaining control of their bottle.

Puff Balloon

6 - 20

Easy

Dining chair, two
different coloured
balloons

10 minutes

*Games with balloons first became
popular during the late nineteenth
century. In 1896 Parker Brothers brought
out a new game called Pillow Dex, which
was a forerunner of Ping Pong. The kit
provided all the ingredients you would
need to volley a balloon across a net
stretched over your parlour table. You
can imagine this more genteel version
of table tennis in action, with Victorian
ladies gently wafting the balloon from
one side of the net to the other. This game is my own addition to the
tradition of balloon games. You might want to use it to build on the
crazy momentum of the Sofa Game; it's equally silly but slightly less
perilous.*

You need two teams with at least three players each. In the
centre of a room place a dining chair. Each team is given
a balloon. On 'Go', the first player in each team sets off to
try and blow their balloon underneath the chair to the
other side. Once successfully blown under, the balloon is
then puffed back directly to the starting line so that the next
player can go. The first team to bring all their members
home wins.

Players aren't allowed to touch an opponent's balloon but

they may blow it. This becomes particularly relevant when the balloons clash on entering the vicinity of the chair. As players scramble to get their balloons under the seat, all sorts of breathy interventions are allowed by the two players fighting it out. Those waiting to race, however, must remain behind the line. The only pressure they're allowed to exert is via cheering.

The Hat Game

6 - 24

Medium

Pens and paper for everyone, hat

1–2 hours

Finally in this section, I would like to share with you the King of Team Games. If there is one game to take from this book, I would like it to be this one. It's like a rich, delicious stew with all your favourite ingredients. It's so versatile and open to so many different ages and levels of skill that everyone seems to be playing it. Indeed, it conforms very well with the theory put forward by the historians and great game collectors Iona and Peter Opie. They argue that, as games become more popular, they begin to attract additional rules, become more elaborate and the length of time needed to play them increases. I believe that this game is relatively recent and has been around in this form for no more than fifteen years or so. It's now very common and, as the following explanation demonstrates, it is still growing and developing.

I learnt the Hat Game when I was touring Russia with The Winter's Tale. *A crowd of us were killing time in a dingy hotel in Minsk when someone suggested this game. There couldn't have been a better place to learn this epic, three-stage event and I've been hooked ever since.*

Begin by giving everyone a pen and a sheet of paper. Everyone tears up their paper to make seven smaller pieces and writes on each a different name of a well-known public figure. The papers are folded and placed in the hat. You will have plenty of names. The group is then divided into two equal teams.

Team A nominates a member of their team to start. They are given a minute – timed by someone on the opposing side – to take names out of the hat and describe the people on the card **without saying their name**. Any name that is correctly guessed the team keeps, so by the end of the minute they have collected a nice pile of names. The hat then passes to the other team who repeat the procedure. The hat goes back and forth until all the names have been guessed. At the end of the round, each team counts the names they have won, records the total and the papers are returned to the hat.

Round two works on the same principle except that now the names are described using **three words only**. For the game to work you must be very strict. 'Ums' and 'ahs' are counted as words. If someone says 'um, ah, celebrity' then that's all they're allowed. No more can be said until the name is guessed. The team may spend the entire minute trying to guess just one name. The stakes are high!

As before, when all the names have been guessed teams tot up their total and all the names go back into the hat. Now is the final showdown. In this round players must act out each name. They can break the name down into syllables, as in Charades, or do a silent impression of the character; becoming for a few priceless seconds Winston Churchill, Marilyn Monroe, Amy Winehouse etc. As acting takes longer than speaking, the time is normally extended for this round, with everyone being given two minutes rather than one.

When the hat has been cleared for the last time, the three totals for each round are added up and the team with the largest number wins.

Stop Press. At the time of writing there are rumours of a **fourth round**. *I have never attempted this but my brother, who is a film director and therefore much more glamorous than me, spent New Year playing the game with some members of the Hollywood crowd (the game's popularity is spreading). They introduced him to this innovation which, he assures me, provides a surreal and hilarious new twist.*

So, for the first time in print:

Players once again remove the names one by one. Now, however, rather than using words or actions, players must make **a single sound**. This sound must embody the essential characteristics of the name on the paper. It might be a low moan, a triumphant roar, a nervous giggle or a stifled sob. Sounds like a challenge, doesn't it?

WORD
GAMES
for WITTY
PEOPLE

Word Games for Witty People

In sixteenth-century France a new vogue for verbal games took hold. These games were played in courtly circles and were known as *jeux d'esprit*. They were part of the burgeoning world of the salon and were played alongside discussions of courtly themes such as love, society and politics. These games reached England via some of the first books of games, such as the anonymously written *The Mysteries of Love and Eloquence* (1658), which describes old word games like Crambo. Many of the games that follow have their beginnings in this early flowering of word games and verbal jousting.

Word games grew in popularity during the nineteenth century and took shape in public events such as the Spelling Bee. 'Bee' was a term that became popular in America during the eighteenth century. It was used to describe events where large numbers of people came together – much like bees – to participate in some communal activity. People would gather to weave, spin, make quilts and, eventually, to compete in spelling matches. The first of these Spelling Bees took place in America during the 1870s. The spelling obsession soon made it across the pond and, in 1876, *The Leisure Hour* reported that 'the walls are placarded with announcements of bees, the newspapers teem with reports of bees, and everybody is talking of bees'. At the same time games based around the alphabet, acrostics, anagrams, word squares and, eventually, crosswords all became big business. It was during this time that the first parlour quiz games arrived, and home quizzes like The World's Educator became all the rage; these games would eventually morph into Trivial Pursuit. These types of word game would also have another very famous descendant, Scrabble.

Scrabble was not invented until the 1930s, when a New York architect, Alfred Mosher Butts, was made redundant in the Depression and decided to invent a game to save his family from poverty. But its roots are clearly to be found in the great flowering of word games during the Victorian age. Indeed, the mathematician, author and games obsessive Lewis Carroll was already moving towards a similar idea. In 1880 he wrote a brief note to himself: 'A game might be made of letters, to be moved about a chess board till they form words.' And then, on New Year's Day 1895, he wrote to a friend:

> If ever you want a light mental recreation, try the '30 letter' puzzle. I tried it for the first time, the other day,

with one of my sisters: and I think it very interesting … Here is our rule. Take 4 or 5 complete alphabets. Put the vowels into one bag, the consonants into another. Shake up. Draw 9 vowels and 21 consonants. With these you must make 6 real words (excluding proper names) so as to use up all the letters. If two people want to do it, then after drawing a set of 30, pick out a set of duplicates for the other player. Sit where you cannot see another's work, and make it a race.

Today, between one and two million Scrabble sets are sold every year, one in three American households owns a set and thirty thousand games are said to begin somewhere in the world every hour. Carroll was on to something.

The games in this chapter are the finest word games to come out of the period from sixteenth-century France to Depression-era America. As befits their roots in the *salon*, they are like after-dinner mints. They benefit from not being rushed and all have an exquisite, cerebral quality as well as being very funny. But before embarking on them, let me share this warning from A. A. Milne:

The initial disadvantage of the paper game is that pencils have to be found for everybody; generally a difficult business. Once they are found, there is no further trouble until the game is over, when the pencils have to be collected from everybody; generally an impossible business. If you are a guest in the house, insist upon a paper game, for it gives you a chance of acquiring a pencil; if you are the host, consider carefully whether you would not rather play a guessing game – A. A. Milne, *Not That It Matters*

Consequences

Consequences is the crazed twin of sensible storytelling. As soon as straight stories were being told, people started delighting in the wrong people doing the wrong things at the wrong time.

3 - 20

Easy

Paper and pens for everyone

1 hour

One of the first examples we have of this kind of game crops up in a play by Ben Jonson called Cynthia's Revels, *which was written in 1600. The game is called 'A Thing Done, and Who Did It' and one of the characters explains the rules like this: 'I imagine, a thing done; Hedon thinks who did it; Moria, with what it was done; Anaides, where it was done; Argurion, when it was done; Amorphus, for what cause it was done; you, Philautia, what followed upon the doing of it; and this gentleman, who would have done it better.'*

The characters then say their suggestions in reverse order, before telling the story from beginning to end; as they do so a joyfully silly tale is revealed. Consequences as we know it starts to appear in games books in the second half of the nineteenth century, now with the addition of pens and paper. As the decades pass, the number of categories gets longer – a man's name, a woman's name, where they met, what happened etc – and, by 1912, players are writing elaborate stories. Here is an example from E. M. Baker's Indoor Games for Children and Young People*:*

Pugnacious Captain Swift, who was dressed in flannels, patent boots, and a silk hat, met dainty Mrs Kruger in a mauve satin petticoat and bathing slippers paddling by moonlight, when he would much rather have met the Duchess of York. They met at Southminster. What he thought was 'How charming she looks with that delicate flush on her fresh young cheeks', but he said, 'Madam, I'm surprised at you.' She thought, 'I wish I'd put on my best hat', but she merely said, 'I'd no idea you were in earnest.' They went for a ride on the Twopenny Tube, and learnt to love one another very dearly. The consequence was she wrote a long letter of complaint to the Queen, and the world said, 'What else could you expect under the circumstances?'

Just as in Blind Man's Buff, this seems another furtive way for the Victorians to have touched on romantic themes forbidden to them in polite conversation. Some years later, one games company, Laughlin Brothers, exploited this market by producing their Elite Conversation Cards. The aim of these was to help prospective couples loosen up by getting witty conversation flowing. The cards were divided between humorous or flirtatious questions and answers. Questions included, 'Have you ever been in love?' which might have been met with 'Why not, I am human.' Another prize example is the delicately put, 'Are you inclined to boss the house?' The Laughlins claimed that the cards 'to bashful people are a great blessing, not only furnishing an hour's amusement, but sometimes leading them to the gates of matrimony'.

Marriage by conversation cards? Times must have been hard.

Everyone is given a pen and paper. Everyone writes at the top an adjective describing a man (for example, 'hunky'). The word is then folded over so that it cannot be read and each paper is passed on to the next person. The name of a man is then written – either someone you know (most fun) or a famous person. This in turn is folded over and passed on. The word 'met' is inserted at this point. Everyone then writes an adjective describing a woman ('gorgeous') and, after that, a woman's name – the papers being folded and passed on after every entry. The next items written are:

The place where they met
What he said to her
What she said to him
What the consequence was
What the world said

The stories are then unfolded and read out, either by each player or by one individual. They are innocent, knowing or blue, depending on the players. But they are always crazy. You can become more ambitious by adding stages. Here is the advanced list:

Adjective for a man
The man
What he was wearing
What he was doing

(Met)

Adjective for a woman

The woman

What she was wearing

What she was doing

Where they met

What he thought

What he said

What she thought

What she said

Where they went

What they did

What the consequence was

What the world said

Variations

There are loads of different games that use the format of Consequences. There are as many versions as ways to tell a story. Here are my two favourites:

Book Reviews

Because you have to write a fair amount during stages of this game, encourage everyone to write small from the beginning to maximize space.

Hand around sheets of lined A4 paper to everyone. Begin by asking everyone to invent a title (*Crimson Nights*, for example) before folding over their paper and passing it on. The next player writes a subtitle (*Or Understanding the New Scottish Parliament*) before folding their paper again and passing it on, the next an author's name (*J. C. Bendon*), the next an extract from the book (*'everywhere they travelled they were met by the haunted stares of those who had gone before, those who had become lost and confused searching for the lost temple of King Solomon'*). After each new entry players fold their papers before passing them round the circle.

For the next entry players write an extract from a review ('*a remarkable feat, the edgy prose is dangerous and concise*') followed by the name of a paper or magazine (*Farming Times*), and then another contrasting review ('*beyond words bad*') followed by the name of second journal (*Northamptonshire Past and Present*). Finally, the papers are unfolded and each player reads out the details of their surreal publication and its critical reception.

Twitter Consequences

The art of twittering demands we become more and more concise. How can we encapsulate the mundane and the miraculous in the shortest number of words? This game teaches you how.

Give everyone playing a sheet of lined A4 paper. Again, you are going to write a fair amount so having lined paper helps people to keep within the available space. Once again, remind people to write small. At the top of their papers ask everyone to write an anecdote of around sixty words, for example:

'The paperboy began his village round at 6.30 that morning. The air was cold and the road icy. Enjoying the thrill of speeding down the hill towards the newsagents, he forgot the wintry conditions and too late slammed on the brakes. As his bike hit a grass verge, he found himself flying into a field of sheep.'

Now everyone passes their paper to the player on their left. After reading the anecdote the next player must shorten the anecdote to thirty words, trying to preserve the essential sense. They may not rearrange the order or add any new words. He or she might write:

'The paperboy began his round at 6.30. Forgetting the icy conditions, he slammed on the brakes. Too late: as his bike hit a verge he found himself flying into sheep.'

Then fifteen words:

'Paperboy forgot icy conditions. His bike hit a verge, he found himself flying into sheep.'

And finally five:

'Paperboy found flying into sheep.'

When everyone has written their five-word summary, they open up their papers and read all their stages out loud. It's fun to go round with everyone reading each equivalent stage as they get shorter and shorter.

Twenty Questions

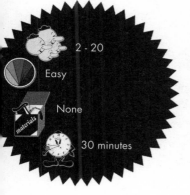

2 - 20

Easy

None

30 minutes

Word games and Radio Four were made for each other. Twenty Questions was the original 'panel game' and the first of its kind to win mass appeal. It was first broadcast on the Home Service – as Radio Four was known originally – in 1947. Before long, the show was attracting fifteen million listeners a week and had become the most popular show on radio. But the game had been around for a long time before its debut on the radio. The games historian Tony Augarde has brought to light this letter from Hannah More, written to her sister on 17 February 1786:

Mrs Fielding and I, like pretty little Misses, diverted ourselves with teaching Sir Joshua and Lord Palmerston the play of twenty questions, and thoroughly did we puzzle them by picking out little obscure insignificant things which we collected from ancient history. Lord North overhearing us, desired to be initiated into this mysterious game, and it was proposed that I should question him: I did so, but his twenty questions were exhausted before he came near the truth. As he at length gave up the point, I told him my thought was the earthen lamp of Epicetus. 'I am quite provoked at my own stupidity,' said his lordship, 'for I quoted that very lamp last night in the

House of Commons' – *The Letters of Hannah More*, ed. R. Brimley Johnson, 1926

The playing company here is pretty elevated and I'm frankly not surprised Lord North didn't guess the 'earthen lamp of Epicetus', even if he had mentioned it in Parliament the night before.

Charles Dickens was also an enthusiast (apparently he managed to guess that the object one of his guests was thinking of was 'the top boot of the left leg of the head post-boy at Newman's Yard, London') and he used the game in A Christmas Carol when Scrooge is shown his nephew playing it at Christmas with his family:

> It was a game called Yes or No, where Scrooge's nephew had to think of something, and the rest must find out what; he was only answering to their questions yes or no, as the case was. The brisk fire of questioning to which he was exposed, elicited from him that he was thinking of an animal, a live animal, a rather disagreeable animal, a savage animal, an animal that growled and grunted sometimes, and talked sometimes, and lived in London, and walked about the streets, and wasn't made a show of, and wasn't led by anyone, and didn't live in a menagerie, was never killed in a market, and was not a horse, or an ass, or a cow, or a bull, or a tiger, or a dog, or a cat, or a bear. At every fresh question that was put to him this nephew burst into a fresh roar of laughter, and was so inexpressibly tickled, that he was obliged to get off the sofa and stamp. At the last the plump sister, falling

into a similar state, cried out:

'I have found it out! I know what it is, Fred! I know what it is!'

'What is it?' cried Fred.

'It's your Uncle Scro-o-o-o-ge!'

Which it certainly was.

This game begins with one player thinking of an object and telling everyone whether it is an 'animal, vegetable or mineral'. 'Animal' refers to anything that is alive, 'vegetable' to any kind of organic matter and 'mineral' to anything else. Everyone then has no more than twenty questions to guess the object.

There is a nice variation called Clumps, when things get more urgent. You have two teams. One member of each team goes out of the room together to agree an object. When they come back they are each interrogated by members of the opposing team. The teams have to discover the mystery object by asking questions which can only be met by 'yes' or 'no'. The fastest team to guess the object wins.

A. A. Milne was a big fan:

> Personally I adore Clumps because of its revelation of hidden talent. There may be a dozen persons in each clump and, in theory, everyone is supposed to take a hand in the cross-examination but in practice it is always one person who extracts the information. Always one person and generally a girl. She has excelled at none of the outdoor games perhaps. She has spoken hardly a word at meals. In our little company she has scarcely seemed to count. But suddenly she wakens into life. In a moment she discovers herself as our natural leader, a leader who we follow humbly. And however we may spend the rest of the time together, the effect of her short hour's triumph will not wholly wear away. She is now established.

A final variation is Botticelli. This game works by someone thinking of a famous person. Let's say, for the sake of convenience, Botticelli. This player then says the first letter of their surname, so in this case 'B'. Everyone sits in a circle and takes it in turn to ask the player in question who they are. They do this indirectly by asking questions about who they are and what they do. So you wouldn't ask, are you Blondie? Instead, you would ask, are you a famous pop star? If Botticelli knows who they are referring to she might say, 'No, I am not Blondie.' But if she doesn't know, and can't think of any pop star with a surname beginning with 'B', then the questioner gets to ask her a direct question, which must be answered truthfully with a yes or no ('Are you alive? Are you a female?' etc). The turn then passes to the next player in the circle, who asks another question (for example, 'Are you a cartoon character? No, I am not Bugs Bunny').

Crucially, Botticelli does not need to know the exact person that the questioner is thinking of. For example, if someone asks, 'Are you a famous composer?', while thinking of Beethoven, then it's fine for Botticelli to answer, 'No, I am not Bach.' Sometimes it's good to ask more specific questions, such as 'Did you compose the Moonlight Sonata?' so that people can't slip through your fingers and you actually establish whether or not someone is Beethoven. The player who guesses Botticelli correctly becomes ON for the next round and thinks of someone else. Needless to say, it's better if this new person's surname starts with a different letter.

Epizootics

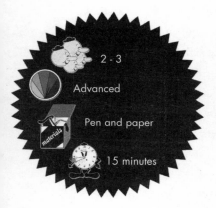

2 - 3

Advanced

Pen and paper

15 minutes

The Danes have a word, hyglig, *which means cosy. I learnt this word from my girlfriend, who is half-Danish and a great fan of the kind of game that is gentle, peaceful and played by candlelight on winter afternoons. This is a game in which the competitive edge is softened and you play simply for the sake of playing. It's a game for two or three people, and one to be played ideally after a warming lunch.*

This is a game for two players or more. Each player draws a grid with twenty-five squares, so you have five boxes across and five down. The first player calls out a letter, for example 'T', which everyone must write down in one of their squares. The next player follows by calling out another letter, which must fill a different square. This process goes on until all the squares have been filled. Letters can be repeated if players wish.

As the letters are called, players have to arrange them within their squares to spell out the maximum number of words they can, horizontally and vertically. The maximum number of words possible is to have ten five-letter words.

The scoring system works like this:

Five-letter words: 10 points

Four-letter words: 5 points

Three-letter words: 3 points

Two-letter words: 1 point

Words included in large ones are not counted and every letter said must go down somewhere on the grid.

My Thought

4 - 10

Advanced

Elastic minds

20 minutes

This game gets the mind working while tickling the funny bone. It's beguiling and gentle and would fare well on Radio Four. There is something artful about its construction that provokes people into being wittier and more inventive than they are normally. It's a wit catalyst.

Everyone sits in a circle. Someone thinks of an object. This person then asks everyone in turn, 'What is my thought like?'

Not having a clue, each person must come up with a response at random: 'Like a dog', 'Like a saucepan', or 'Like roller skates'. After collecting everyone's answers, the player reveals the object he or she was thinking of. Everyone must now explain, in turn, how this object is like the thing they volunteered. The fun lies in the merit of the explanations.

Let's say the object was a harp. When asked why a harp is like a dog, the first player might reply, 'Because it makes strange sounds when it's plucked', and the second might answer that 'A saucepan is like a harp because you hold both in your hands'. The third might claim a harp is like 'roller skates, because both of them take you to faraway places'. The player with the most ingenious explanation wins.

Taboo

3 - 7

Moderate

Just players

10 minutes

This has the quality of a zany quiz and works with a small group. It's another member of that family of games where, through asking quick-fire questions, you are trying to compel people to say the forbidden word or phrase.

Someone takes on the role of quizmaster and begins the game by declaring a letter that is taboo. The quizmaster can choose any letter in the alphabet but it works best if he or she chooses a vowel to begin with. This player now asks everyone questions which they must answer in sentences, *but without using the taboo letter*. Hesitation is forbidden and the quizmaster can leap around the circle firing off questions to anyone he chooses. The quizmaster continues until everyone eventually crumbles and the first player who is out becomes the new quizmaster.

Let me share an example. Let's say that the letter 'a' is taboo. So some questions and answers might go like this:

Quizmaster: How did you get here tonight?

Player 1: I drove.

Quizmaster: Did you enjoy your supper?

Player 2: Yes, quite delicious.

Quizmaster: What's your name?

Player 3: Mary.

Player 3 goes out and the game continues.

With all these high-pressure, maverick word games if you are the quizmaster don't give your targets time to think. And don't allow people to reply with just one-word sentences!

Sausages

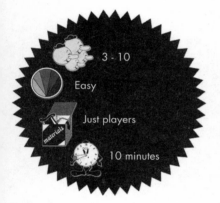

3 - 10

Easy

Just players

10 minutes

This game is definitely in the silly division. One player acts as interrogator. Her simple job is to ask all the other players questions to which they must always answer 'sausages'. As soon as they laugh (or even smile, if you want to be really hardcore) they go out. You want to balance mundane and ridiculous questions from 'What do you fry that's made of pork?' to 'What is your mother's maiden name?'

You can, of course, replace 'sausages' with any answer that tickles your particular fancy, the sillier the better. 'Singer-songwriter Elaine Paige', works pretty well, as does 'baked beans'.

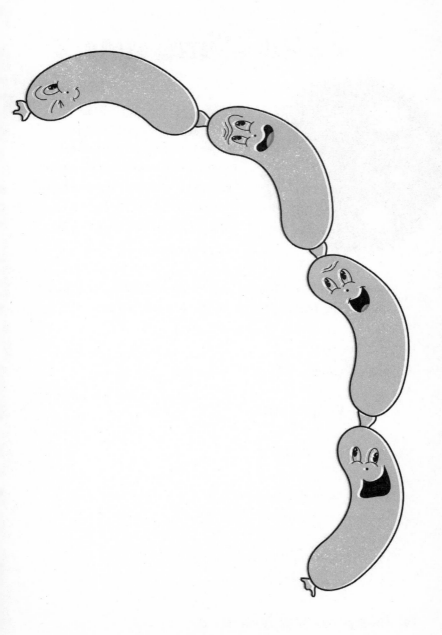

How, When, Where?

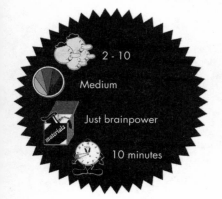

2 - 10

Medium

Just brainpower

10 minutes

You can play this game very happily in a pair as well as in a group. It has a naughty edge, which I have no idea whether the Victorians were aware of. It certainly seems to be a favourite, coming up many times in games books throughout the nineteenth century.

Somebody leaves the room. Everyone else thinks of an object. The player returns and has to ask different people in the room, these three questions:

How do you like it?

When do you like it?

Where do you like it?

Players have to answer as best they can in relation to the object everyone has chosen.

An example of an exchange might be:

How do you like it?

Accurately.

Where do you like it?

Against the wall.

When do you like it?

All the time.

The player can guess the object at any point. You've probably guessed that the example here is a clock. However, if the questioner remains stumped he can keep asking the same three questions, with people providing different information each time. The secret is to keep the answers cryptic enough for the guessing to take some time.

Fictionary Dictionary

3 - 12

Medium

Pen and paper for everyone, dictionary

45 minutes

For my twenty-seventh birthday I was given a second-hand copy of the Oxford English Dictionary in two volumes. What seemed like a rather dry birthday gift proved a gamester's dream. Living in Northampton, on the second floor of a Victorian house called Toad Hall, I had many hours of joy exploring the barmier reaches of the English language. Just opening the dictionary and sharing bizarre definitions was pleasure enough.

One of the most enduring and popular of all modern games has been created on this very principle: Call My Bluff. This is the version I played in Toad Hall.

Someone is appointed umpire. They take a dictionary (the older and dustier the better) and choose an unusual word. They read out this word and the other players have to write down their fantastical definitions one by one, before popping them into a hat. The umpire writes down the actual definition and throws this into the hat, too. The umpire then pulls out the papers one by one, reading each definition aloud. When they have heard all the options, players must choose the one they think is the authentic definition. Players who guess the true meaning are given one point and you also get a point for any player who thinks your definition is the right one (this counts for the umpire, too). Play a few rounds, varying the umpire role, and then total up the points. The person with the most points wins.

Let's take the example of the word **caratch**. Five potential definitions are:

A rush basket used to pack tobacco in.

The side wall of a tent.

The tribute levied by Turks on their Christian subjects.

An iron collar used for punishment.

A genus of bird, related to the ostrich, whose wings are useless for flight, native to South-East Asia.

The answer is number three. *Caratch* is an Arabic word, dates from 1684 and was indeed a tax on Christians.

Ex Libris

4 - 12

Advanced

Pens, paper, hat, shelf of books

1 hour

This is an advanced game for wannabe authors. You need a good collection of books on hand and people who are very up for it. I know people who live in fear of playing this game and others who spend entire weekends doing nothing else. You can buy this as a board game, but why pay money when you can create your own DIY version?

Someone begins by choosing a book. They will be the umpire for this round. Let's say the book is *Sons and Lovers* by D. H. Lawrence. Everyone has a pen and paper. When the book has been chosen everyone writes their best idea of what the first line of the book might sound like. So, in this case, you might write something like, 'Amongst the falling soot of the evening, Aunt Mary began her long walk home.' Everyone writes their suggestions down and puts them into a hat. At the same time the umpire writes down the actual opening sentence and throws it into the hat, too. When everyone has submitted their suggestion, all the entries are taken out of the hat and read out by the umpire.

Everyone now votes for what they think is the real opening line. You get one point for choosing the true version and one point for all those who vote for your untrue version. You can keep going, with different people taking it in turns to be the umpire, until your brain melts and a winner is declared.

The actual first line of *Sons and Lovers* is:

'The Bottoms' succeeded to *'Hell Row.'*

So, it's not as easy as you might think.

Maggot

Unlimited

Absurdly easy

None

Endless

There is an entire category of games that are self-consciously ridiculous, but their stupidity is the key to their success.

For this game you replace a word in a book title with the word *maggot*. You are looking for the most incongruous change. As people think of examples they simply shout them out. And that's it. My favourites include *Bleak Maggot*, *To the Maggot* and *The Satanic Maggot*. It's good to keep the word singular, so there's even more incongruity when it's transplanted into a sentence.

But be wary: although completely stupid, this game really can go on for hours!

Douche!

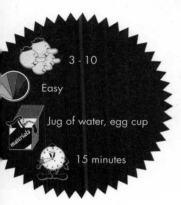

3 - 10

Easy

Jug of water, egg cup

15 minutes

Here is another wacky game which seems to be gaining in popularity at the moment. You can use a thimble or shot glass to hold the water but I think an egg cup works best.

Sitting round the table a 'doucher' is chosen. This person must propose a category with a limited number of examples and which is not too esoteric. The films of Tom Cruise is a good category to start with. The doucher 'locks' an example of this category into her mind (you can ask her to write it down but it seems a bit untrusting).

After filling the egg cup with water, the doucher holds it over the head of each player at a time and asks them to give an example of the category. In this case they might say *Top Gun, Days of Thunder, Rain Man* etc (the list is pretty long). As soon as someone says the example in the doucher's mind they are 'douched' with the contents of the egg cup.

The soggy victim now takes over the role of doucher and proposes a new category.

You can play this game in two different gears. You can either play fast, with 'douching' for hesitations as well, or you can go for the agonizingly slow version. This involves the doucher leaving a lengthy, sweat-inducing pause after each answer before moving on or delivering a soaking. I prefer the latter.

Games for the Great Outdoors

The Eel's Foot

When I was growing up, every June we would go camping with two other families. The mums stayed at home and the dads were in charge. Each year we would camp in the same field in Suffolk next to a pub called the Eel's Foot. It wasn't a camping site in the conventional sense of the word; it was just a large field with a tumbledown, corrugated iron shack at one end. That was the lavatory.

The other two families were neater than us and had much smarter tents. As they put theirs up with minimum fuss, our more ramshackle affair took ages and was accompanied by much swearing from Dad, as he shouted at us to 'hold that bloody pole straight!' Our tent was only made for four so my two brothers, sister and I huddled in the inner section, and Dad would have to sleep in the 'hall' next to the cold box, garden furniture and barbecue. He would sit out late into the night drinking with the other dads, claiming that the only way he could sleep was by getting plastered first. We would hear him stumbling around before he collapsed onto his narrow camp bed.

One of the families had a trio of beautiful daughters. They always emerged from their tent impeccably turned out, and talking to them made us feel nervous and shabby. In a desperate attempt to hide our mutual shyness we would find games to play together. In these moments of running and catching our nerves were briefly forgotten and we were able to do something together, to play, in these early summer evenings, as a group; one charged with the faint presence of desire.

In this section I am going to share some games that you will probably recognize from your own childhood but which still have the potential to be enormous fun. They are all designed to be played outdoors. The amount of space they need varies: for some you just need a small yard, and others would benefit from a field or park. For all these games it's important to define your playing area. Football really took off when someone decided to mark out the pitch and all these games need the intensity of physical parameters. Marking out the four corners with piles of coats or bags will also help prevent complete exhaustion.

Here are two old-fashioned playground games to start with:

Gaps

6 - 30

Easy

Large playing area

15 minutes

You're at a barbecue or picnic. Lunch is over, you've had a few drinks – what now? Let's play a game! Games like this one are good to get people on their feet and running around. If you can manage to convince a crowd to have a go then you'll have a riot. All ages can play games like this and they work particularly well when adults have to race children, and teenagers have to compete against their fortysomething parents.

Everyone stands in a circle except one person who is ON. This person runs rounds the ring and touches the back of one of the players in the circle. They both set off running immediately in opposite directions, trying to be the first to reach the gap made in the circle by the player who was touched. The one who reaches the gap first stays in the circle, while the other one becomes ON.

Tierce

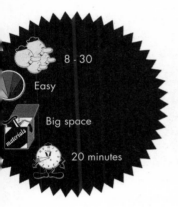

8 - 30

Easy

materials

Big space

20 minutes

The name of this ancient game comes from the Old French word meaning three. The word and the game were introduced to England by Norman soldiers at the time of William the Conqueror. Children and adults have been playing it ever since.

Everyone, apart from one pair, forms a large ring, standing in twos, one behind another. The two outside the ring stand slightly apart. One is the Chaser and one is the Chased. The game begins when the Chased attempts to take up position (if he can do so before the Chaser grabs him) in front of one of the couples in the ring, thus making three. As soon as he does so he is safe and the player at the back of the little group now has to run. When they are caught they become the Chaser, while the one doing the catching becomes the Chased until he gets to safety and forces that role onto another.

Chain Gang

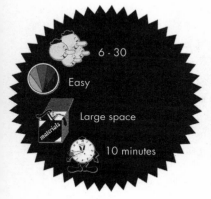

6 - 30

Easy

Large space

10 minutes

I learnt this game at school during PE. Playing it was a relief because it meant a break from the horrors of vaulting over the horse and climbing up ropes.

Mark your space out. The more players you have the bigger the space you need. But don't go crazy as a smaller space is good for heightening the tension. Someone is ON and begins to chase everybody else. As people are caught they join hands with the catcher to form an ever lengthening 'chain' of chasers. Only those at the end of lines can tag people. If your space is very wide and the line is becoming too unwieldy then you can break off into small chains of two or four. In the gym it was fun as the chain was eventually wide enough to span the room. You had to get from one end to another, climbing under the legs of players before those on the end could grab you.

The Secret Life of Balls

Games where you muck about with a ball are older than recorded history. Scenes of ball games were depicted on the walls of Egyptian tombs dating from before 2000 BC. And the Romans enjoyed a ball game called Trigon. In this game three people would stand at the three points of a triangle drawn in the sand. The fun lay in throwing balls at each other without warning and trying to keep three balls in the air at any one moment, with slaves acting as ball boys.

In ancient Greece ball play was elevated into a dance known as Nausikaa. This was a special kind of ball dance that you can see depicted on the sides of vases and pots. The ball dance has since fallen away but, as the philosopher Roger Caillois has argued, it has left a definite trace in European languages where ball (*balla* in low Latin) has come to mean dance. In Italian there is *ballare*, and in English we have ball. The idea remains even in the word of the song that once accompanied the dance, in the Italian *balleta*, French *bal* and the English ballad.

The idea of balls being linked to religion and spirituality

also has a forgotten place in church ceremonies. Here is a fascinating glimpse of a long neglected marriage between God and games.

The following describes a ritual held in a monastery in Auxerre. New recruits to the order had to bring a ball with them:

> The dean or his representative, who is dressed like all those present in the cowl, receives the ball from one who is newly baptized or from a newly admitted cleric. All sing the antiphon appropriate to the song of Easter. Then the dean seizes the ball with his left hand and paces solemnly in time to the music. The others join hands and dance around the master. While they are dancing, the dean throws the ball to individual dancers in turn and they throw it back. The game proceeds to the accompaniment of the organ and the dance. When song and dance are ended, the company goes to lunch.
>
> *Western Folklore* VII (1948), 157

This description reflects something of the euphoric nature of ball play. Knowing how binding and frankly joyous throwing a ball around can be, this account seems to hark back to a time when religion seemed to be in touch with a more playful, even euphoric side of itself.

Before attempting anything complicated, it's good to begin simply by just throwing the ball to each other in a circle. This gives people the chance to practise throwing and catching in a stress-free way and allows you to remind people about the importance of eye contact between thrower and catcher.

Broken Bottles

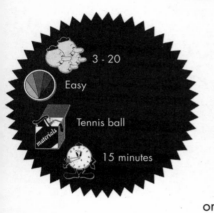

3 - 20

Easy

Tennis ball

15 minutes

This is a catching game with penalties for missed catches. Like the Romans, you can play with a minimum of three or with many more. If you fail to catch the ball you have to forfeit some part of your body. First you have to hold one hand behind your back, next stand on one leg, then go down on one knee, then two knees and, finally, out you go.

Donkey

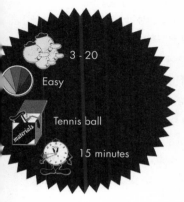

3 - 20

Easy

Tennis ball

15 minutes

This game does not involve any loss of body parts. Once again you throw the ball around the circle. This time, if you drop the ball you are called 'D'. When you drop the ball again you become 'DO'. With each subsequent dropped ball you acquire another letter. Finally, when your letters spell DONKEY, you're out.

Another even simpler and more explosive variant is Bombs – everyone stands in a circle. If you drop the ball you have to explode.

Pig in the Middle

3 - 10

Easy

Tennis ball

15 minutes

This game, also known as Fool in the Middle or, in Lancashire, Mug in t'Middle, is known by everyone. Three players stand in a line. The one in the middle tries to intercept the ball as it's thrown between the two other players. The thrower who allows the ball to be lost becomes the pig.

I am including this game to share with you a simple but very fun twist. Try playing it on the move, with all three of you running as the ball is thrown – ideally along the beach. It transforms the game from something static into a high-energy, exhilarating experience.

The Pattern Game

5 - 20

Advanced

Three differently coloured balls

30 minutes

As a kid in the playground I was intrigued by games played only by girls. As boys careered around feigning American accents and driving imaginary squad cars, girls would be patiently absorbed in intricate skipping games, clapping games with elaborate rhymes and lengthy versions of Cat's Cradle. I remember watching these games while eating my packet of crisps and realizing that they really took some skill. Unlike shouting, driving and dying, they required patience and dexterity and they induced a mood quite different from the frenzied fights of the boys.

This game comes from the Circus Space, a school that trains young circus performers. Jugglers and acrobats use this game as a warm-up to tune in with each other before a performance. You can play it just as easily with a group of friends. But you need to lead it confidently since it's easy for everyone to become very confused. If you can make it work, you will have shared something truly special.

You need three differently coloured balls. Most sports shops sell tennis balls in different colours but soft juggling balls also work very well. You begin with everyone standing in a circle. After you have thrown the ball around randomly for a while to get everyone's concentration, you can start making your first pattern. With your first ball throw the ball from one player to another across the circle. When they get the ball a player throws it to someone who hasn't had it yet, so everyone has caught the ball once and thrown it once. Always begin and end your pattern with the same person.

Let's take an example. With a group of five players – Simon, Olivia, Sebastian, Emma and Daniel – your first pattern might be:

Pattern One (Red Ball)

Simon to Olivia

Olivia to Sebastian

Sebastian to Emma

Emma to Daniel

Daniel to Simon

After you have established this pattern, stop and ask everyone to point at who they throw to in this sequence. Ask everyone to look at who is throwing to them and who they throw to. Memorize this and then go through the sequence a couple more times, so that it has really sunk in.

Now you are ready for the second pattern. Remember that the same person always begins and ends the sequence. Using the second, differently coloured ball, your new pattern might go:

Pattern Two (Yellow Ball)

Simon to Sebastian

Sebastian to Daniel

Daniel to Olivia

Olivia to Emma

Emma to Simon

Once more, ask everyone to point at who they are throwing to. Absorb these positions and practise the sequence a few more times. As the leader you have to judge when people have really memorized the journey of the ball. When you are convinced that everyone has got the second pattern down, go back to pattern one. When this is flowing well – and don't rush it – add the second ball so now people are throwing two different balls in two different sequences. It's normal that people in the circle might have two balls being thrown at them at the same time. This is fine. There is no rush: just encourage everyone to throw the ball only when the catcher is ready.

If you can manage two sequences at the same time you are doing really well and all players should feel the vibe of everyone's shared concentration. If you feel people are ready to move on, take the first two balls out of circulation and introduce the third pattern. This pattern should be different again and might go:

Pattern Three (Blue Ball)

Simon to Emma

Emma to Sebastian

Sebastian to Daniel

Daniel to Olivia

Olivia to Simon

Ask everyone to point at who they throw the ball to. Repeat this process for patterns one and two. Now you are going to go for the triple. Begin by establishing pattern one, then, after a few minutes (again, don't rush this), establish pattern two and then finally bring in pattern three. The different colours of each ball will help you to remember which ball should be thrown to which person.

The challenge here is to engage the body's intuition. Thinking won't help you; you have to let your body remember the sequences and let it do the work. If you can sustain three patterns you will feel euphoric.

Cirque du Soleil is not far off.

Echo

6 - 30

Medium (you have to be good at throwing)

Ball, building

20 minutes

This is a very old game that was still being played in the North Country up until the 1950s and 1960s. The game originated from the simple thrill of trying to throw a ball as high as possible over a building. Recently, I set out with a bunch of friends on a camping holiday to try the game out. We had some problems finding the right sort of building. The game was first played in rural areas where the kind of long, narrow barns you needed were common. These aren't that easy to find now. In the end we had to settle for a hexagonal building that was built as an observation point above a beach. The game was made more difficult to play by the building having a kind of steeple and by high winds.

Despite these obstacles, the game's strength emerged intact. The primary fun lies in waiting with your team on one side of the building and not being able to see the opposing team. You are waiting for the ball to fly over the roof at any point. Success lies in speed of response and placing your players in the right positions to cover all catching possibilities.

The game is played in two teams. Each team stands on different sides of the building. One person throws a tennis ball over the roof and calls out a warning cry as he does so. If someone on the opposing team manages to catch it she runs round to the other side of the building and throws it at one of her opponents. If that person is hit he has to return with the thrower as her prisoner. The aim of the game is to keep going until one team becomes completely enslaved by the other.

Bit like life.

The Challenge Walk

Sunday mornings were always the same. After finishing my paper round, which took twice as long as on weekdays, I would come home to find Mum still in bed and Dad making boiled eggs. My two brothers would stagger out of bed and we would prepare for our weekly games ritual: the Challenge Walk. After raiding the airing cupboard for extra thick socks and squeezing into wellingtons, we would all pile into the car with Chuck, our black cocker spaniel. Once on the road, Dad played heavy rock on the car stereo, to get him in the mood. We would sit quietly in the back, contemplating the challenges to come.

We would drive out of St Albans through the small village of Sandridge and into the countryside beyond. Crossing a small ford, we would climb a vertiginous lane, bounded with high hedges, eventually reaching open countryside. After we'd climbed the gate into the first field, the Challenge Walk would begin.

The first stretch of the walk was along an abandoned railway line, flanked on both sides by steep slopes. To reach the next leg, you had to climb up one of these slopes to reach a path snaking through the next field. And so the first challenge was simple – you had to be the first to make the ascent. The ground was always muddy and there was little to grab on to for support. To reach the top you had to dig your hands and feet firmly into the dirt and drag yourself up. And you would be attacked as you climbed. We were all highly competitive and there were often fierce struggles. You had to tread a strategic path between hauling yourself up and pushing back any close competitors. We became locked in prolonged fights to dislodge one another's hands or feet from the slim branch they were clutching. One Sunday I remember my eldest brother managing to unclasp my dad's hand from a solitary branch, and feeling a primal, forbidden pleasure as I watched him tumble down the slope, arriving face down on the muddy path. But there was no space for pity; another's fall was your opportunity for victory. The mud was a democratizing presence – it didn't matter how strong or big you were, you needed an ingenious mixture of guile, luck and speed to win.

But this was only stage one. Caked in mud and nursing vendettas, we would race along bridleways, battle our way across wooded ravines and test our throwing skills by hurling stones at gateposts. The aim was to accrue as many points as possible and be declared that week's winner.

Games have traditionally included tests of strength and skill. The Challenge Walk was a makeshift selection of just such games. Landscape was the provocation and spontaneity was the key. Although the games could be fraught or violent they were a thrilling way to engage with each other and the world around us.

Battle for the Banner

8 - 26

Medium
(it's a bit rough)

Something to act as the
banner, big space

30 minutes

Between the ages of eight and eleven,
Wednesday evening meant one thing for
me: Cubs. It seems strange to remember
the raising and lowering of the Union
Jack at the beginning and end of every
class, the towering late middle-aged,
bearded men in brown shirts, the singing
of the national anthem and a very itchy
green jumper. But, among the sweat and
hysteria of a crowd of thirty boys, I learnt
how to play some excellent games.

Many of these had a gladiatorial quality about them and included a
degree of physical violence. I remember 'hopping duels', where,
keeping your arms folded and hopping on one leg, you had to force
your opponent to lose their balance by a process of vigorous bumping.
Such games reached their peak during the annual Cub Camp. After
roasting dough twists by the fire, carving thumb sticks and making
clandestine visits to the site tuck shop, we would play 'wide games'.
These were known as such because they were played over large
outdoor spaces. They were games on a grand scale when an entire
forest or hill became your playground. Rough and tumble was
encouraged and I played them with a heady mix of terror and
exhilaration.

I recently played this game again and it's still good fun played with
two teams of people in their thirties. It's your chance to become a ten-
minute hero.

Team A erects a banner. This could be someone's jumper or shirt stuck on top of a tent pole or sturdy branch. This is firmly rooted in the earth on a raised area of ground. A hillock is the best place, somewhere where the banner can be stormed from all sides, but otherwise a wide space that has a soft grass or sand surface is fine. Team A begins by becoming the guardians of the banner. They must taunt and jeer at the other team. Team B responds by waging their campaign to seize the banner.

The rules are few but exacting. Pushing, pulling, wrestling, bumping, shouldering and tackling are allowed. Punching, kicking and hair pulling are not. There are also various ways, both simple and complex, of establishing how players 'die'.

One rule is that as soon as someone is forced to the floor they are 'dead' and must retire to the sidelines. A more complex technique, which I learnt at Cubs, is that everyone has a circle of thread tied around their upper arm: Team A in red and Team B in white. These threads are tied tightly so that they stay in place as people run around. Once this lifeline of thread is grabbed and broken by an opposing player the player must bow out. If you have plenty of players, some of whom are averse to fighting, you can install a Red Cross Station. This is a neutral area where players can go and have their threads replaced. Players might have the chance of one or two extra lives.

The game continues until the banner is won or the attacking team has effectively been killed off by the defenders. You might want to introduce a time limit; for example, giving a team twenty minutes to storm the banner before the roles are reversed. Military strategies are useful: flanking, tactical withdrawals, double bluffs and surprise assaults are all worth remembering.

Crumbs and Crusts

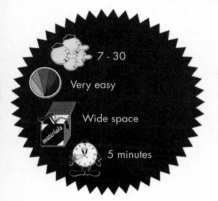

7 - 30

Very easy

Wide space

materials

5 minutes

Alongside challenges of physical dexterity or metal ingenuity there is a class of game that depends purely on chance. I am thinking of games played with dice or gambling games like roulette or even our very own National Lottery. These are games that require you to do nothing but guess. And there is no ambiguity. You either win or lose. I would like to share this game with you because, as well as being fun, it provides a fascinating glimpse into the origins of Heads and Tails.

Everyone is divided into teams, which have to stand facing each other very close. Eight metres behind each team is a line of coats. One team is called the Crumbs and the other is called the Crusts. One player stands to the side as the umpire. When both teams are ready, the umpire, after a dramatic pause, calls out the name of one of the teams. This team must try and catch as many of the opposing team as they can before they reach their home line. The fun comes in the moment of blind panic during the seconds after the call has been made and people are trying to compute whether they should flee or grab. As you play a number of rounds you can keep tally of how many people make it home and how many are caught, translating this into points for each team.

The Opies have traced this game back to an ancient Greek pastime called Ostrakinda, meaning 'The Game of the Shell'. The Greek writer Pollux describes how boys took a shell and smeared one side with pitch, which they called 'Night', while the other side of the shell, the one that remained white, they called 'Day'. Players would form two teams, one being Day and the other Night. The two teams faced each other as an umpire threw the shell up. If the shell fell to the ground pitch side up, Night had to chase Day or the other way around. Anyone caught was called an ass and had to allow his catcher to ride on his back. The game caught on throughout the Roman Empire and, by the second century AD, the phrase 'at the turn of a shell' had become popular.

In England the game pops up again as Cross and Pile, where the shell had become a coin. The Cross was the English coat of arms and the Pile was the King's face. Edward II was a great fan. In one of his accounts is written: 'Item paid to Henry, the King's barber, for money which he lent to the king to play at Cross and Pile. Five shillings. Item, paid to Pires Bernard, usher of the King's chamber, money which he lent the king and which he lost at Cross and Pile.'

And then the game resurfaces as Crusts and Crumbs, while Cross and Pile becomes Heads or Tails. To bring all these traditions together I would suggest calling the two teams Heads or Tails and the caller throwing a coin to declare who should chase whom.

Manhunt

6 - 20

Medium (there's a fair amount of running around)

Stamina

45 minutes

It's always amazing to discover how a game that you played as a child, and thought was your own, actually comes from somewhere else. Recently, I discovered The Weekend Book, a book that was originally published in 1924 before being reprinted many times up until the 1950s. It's a compendium of things to do at the weekends and includes poems, recipes, tips on good excursions as well as a section on games. Reading through it, there was Manhunt.

The game was conceived for adults, and fit ones at that. It suggests playing the game over a massive area 'six miles by one' and advises that you establish your boundaries on a map, with a pub as your end point. The aim is for one team to make it to the pub without being caught by the others. The hunters are given a fifteen-minute head start to hide and create ambushes (they may not congregate around the starting line) before the two or three other players set out to reach the pub without being captured. The author suggests having lunch at the pub before reversing the teams and 'manhunting home'. The instructions end with a warning, advising potential players that the game is 'unsuitable for crowded suburban areas'. I would second this. People being wrestled to the ground outside Boots, while trying to reach the White Hart, might be profoundly unsettling for the locals.

For this game you ideally need a very large area, especially if you are playing with eight or more players. Before you start, establish your boundaries but allow yourself a good half a mile or so radius. Ideally, you want a landscape that combines open space – such as a playing field or common – with places to hide like trees or small buildings. However, the game is so flexible that it will work wherever you are – be it at the edge of a campsite or in an urban park.

One person is ON. He counts to thirty while everyone else runs to hide. When the counting is done, this player opens his eyes and goes off to look for everyone else.

There is no base to return to in this game. Instead, the player who is ON must find and touch another player. When he manages to do so, this player then joins the opposing team. Gradually, the task becomes easier as more and more people are found and join the hunters. It's great scouring the site to discover the last few people, until finally a dramatic chase ensues when it ends up with one last player against the rest.

Playing on the Street

The travel writer Norman Douglas was passionate about games that developed in cities. He was interested in games that appeared in response to the urban landscape and was fascinated by street games. In the first decade of the twentieth century he scoured the streets of pre-First World War London talking to kids and recording their games. His book *London Street Games* was published in 1916 and is full of verbatim interviews with kids about games they loved playing. The style and language of the kids seems strikingly remote. Here is one passage in which a group of kids try to explain what happened when some of their gang disagreed during a game of Cops and Robbers:

'D'ye want a claht over the jor?' says one. 'Cos yer never did touch me 'ead, so there.'

'Ole Ikey see'd me doos it.'

'Liar. Cos 'e wos t'ovver side o'the street.'

'E never. Yer wos on the grahnd when I crahned yer napper.'

'Liar. Yer sez I wos a-layin dahn when all the time I wos on me stumps. Yer finks I'm up the pole to 'ear yer tork. Knock 'arf yer fice orff.'

'Ef yer want an eye bunged up or a punch on the snaht –'

'Well ef I'm a liar yo're the biggest. So yer lumps it. I'm goin to be blowed ef I play wiv a lahsy blisterin blitherin blinkin blightin bloomin bleedin blasted barstard wot's got a mover wot's gota a bloke wot's –'

'Ere, d'ye want a clip on the Kiber-pass?'

For those kids the city was the ultimate playground – forgotten tunnels, disused railway lines, crumbling parks and overgrown cemeteries. Their games were a secret history of the city; a hidden network of chants, rules and sayings. In his book Douglas gives us a glimpse into this urban folklore of games.

Ting Tang Tommy

4 - 20

Medium (you have to be able to run fast)

Wide outdoor space

45 minutes

Douglas writes about the game that gives this book its title and which was one of the first games I remember playing. It grew up in the streets of London before the First World War and its original name was Tin Can Copper, in reference to the tin can that served as a base. When you made it back without being caught by the person on guard, you would kick the can as a way of declaring yourself home.

I first played it on the street with the Club and I've been playing it ever since. Its popularity across the country is shown by the many names it travels under: among them Block, Forty-Forty and Chocky 1-2-3. Here are the rules as I remember them from playing it in the Brickie twenty-five years ago.

One player stays at the base, covers his eyes and counts down from fifty, while everyone else runs off and hides. On reaching zero the player shouts, 'Coming, ready or not!' and sets out to look for the others. As soon as he sees someone he runs back to base and calls out their name and whereabouts, for example, 'Ting Tang Tommy, I see Helen behind the swings!' This person must then leave their hiding place and return to the base, a prisoner.

IIf, however, the person who is seen makes it back to the camp first or, indeed, makes it back to the camp without being seen at all, then they call, 'Ting Tang Tommy Home' and are now safe.

In some versions if a player makes it back successfully then everyone else who has been captured is freed to hide once again. But I think this approach is too demoralizing for the player doing the looking. I think it works best by being a game in which you are trying to reach home safely.

In the Forest

When I was working at the Royal Theatre in Northampton I directed pantomimes, shows that toured village halls and revivals of popular plays by writers like Alan Bennett and Alan Ayckbourn. But after four years in the job I was beginning to feel restless. I needed something new.

For ages I had been intrigued by the Polish style of making theatre. I'd heard a lot about their physical, uncompromising, script-free approach. I wanted to break free from the constraints of the proscenium arch and re-find my passion for theatre. I spoke to my boss and persuaded him to give me a modest amount of money to establish a small, determined team of teenagers, who I would take to Poland for a crack, commando training in creating theatre – Polish style.

I spent a month going around Northamptonshire holding auditions to recruit my team. Although my enthusiasm was unbounded, it wasn't shared by the local actors. As I travelled around youth clubs, parish halls and leisure centres, attendance was poor. Despite having advertised the auditions in local papers and through an e-mail campaign, I would often arrive to discover two or three teenagers, accompanied by an anxious looking parent,

keen to ask me if this was the best way of getting an
agent. The weeks wore on and I became increasingly
dispirited about finding my team; where were the bold,
adventure-seeking young actors that I craved?

One rainy Saturday morning I arrived at the Castle Theatre
in Wellingborough. The town was grey and unwelcoming
and I was seriously questioning my endeavour. Wouldn't it
be best to run back to the welcoming arms of *Bedroom
Farce*? I walked round the foyer, assessing who might be
around for the audition. There was the barman, an elderly
couple having a Coke and a young mother feeding her
toddler an early lunch. Today I would have no one. Just
after eleven, when I was turning off the lights, a short,
thick-set young man in a black vest arrived. I presumed
that he worked backstage so I murmured my farewells and
made for the door. 'Is this the audition?' he asked gruffly.
'Yes,' I replied, feeling distinctly embarrassed about the
undeniable lack of participants. 'Tell me more,' he said.

'Ratty' became my first recruit. His edgy persona set the
tone. Gradually, I began to find people who had dropped
out of the system. I met a girl working as a singer in the
local nightclub; another boy was covering shifts part-time
in the theatre box office; another had left school and was
working in a hardware shop. Rather than seeking stardom,
these people were linked by a determination to uncover

unusual, unconventional experiences. After two months of scouring the county, I had my company of fifteen participants. We were ready to make the journey.

A small coach picked us up at Kraków airport and drove us through the night to Brezinka, a tumbledown farmhouse in the middle of a huge pine forest. As we unloaded our bags and the snow began to fall, we were taken to the accommodation block – two large rooms where we unrolled our sleeping bags directly onto the floor. Our Polish hosts were welcoming but matter-of-fact. Blowing up my travel pillow and looking at the faces of my young companions, I sensed their unease. No beds or even bunks. Exhausted from the journey, we lay down on the hard floor and fell asleep.

Our first morning began with extreme acrobatics. There was one problem. I couldn't do any of them. The Poles insisted that I participate in all the activities. I had readily agreed to this via e-mails sent from my cosy office in Northampton. But now, standing in my old track suit bottoms in a Polish forest being asked to do a cartwheel, I began to have serious reservations. At school I'd found even head over heels beyond me, so now I feigned a headache and ushered the teenagers onwards. It proved an unrelenting regime. Acrobatics were followed by singing, which was followed by more acrobatics, which was followed by more singing, followed by supper. All the rooms were heated only by wood-burning stoves so, in the breaks, we had to chop and distribute logs around the site. After supper there was more singing and acrobatics, culminating in acrobatics while singing.

As the week went on, the group began to realize that my prowess in physical theatre was not quite what I had claimed. As I tried to maintain my dignity during my third attempt at a backward roll, I was aware that I was fast becoming the butt of everyone's jokes. However, they were struggling, too. By day three exhaustion and homesickness was beginning to set in. So it was with some alarm that we greeted the news that the night-running sessions were to begin that evening.

Wearing all the layers we could find, we gathered outside our accommodation block in the encroaching darkness. Snowflakes were beginning to fall through the fading light. There was a strange, eerie feeling of expectation as we waited to begin. Four of the Poles arrived, two carrying flaming torches to light our way. This added to the feeling of a ritual about to take place, an event somehow out of time. We set off in a huddle through the wood. The pace was set by two Poles running out at the front. We began gently and were directed to run in threes, arm in arm.

After a few minutes, the Poles gestured that the runner in the middle should turn around, to run backwards supported by their partners on both sides. I found myself being turned around and running backwards, watching the path fall away. Being carried along, I was momentarily free to look up and watch the stars beckon to me from above.

As we began to go deeper into the woods more and more extraordinary things began to happen. Sometimes we ran in single file following the leader, zigzagging through the tree trunks and leaping one by one over a frozen brook. Sometimes we would clasp hands to form a single line of runners weaving our way through the forest. Having struggled all week to overcome my physical fears, here, in this playful context, with no time to think or anticipate, I rediscovered a feeling of courage and freedom. As we ducked under branches and leapt across fallen pines, I realized that this was another version of the Challenge Walk. The Poles, who trained regularly in this way, were sharing with us their way of playing, of creating games inspired by their landscape.

That night there was a new calm in the dormitories. We no longer noticed the hard floors and the rest of the week passed quickly. When I got back to Northampton I realized that life didn't need to be a walk in the park. It could be a run in the forest.

It was time to move on.

Everything You Need for a Rainy Day

Traditionally, games have been played on Sunday in lieu of anything much else to do. Sunday was established as the Sabbath by the Puritans who banned plays, public music and dancing and heavily restricted any kind of trading. 'Is anything in the world so wearisome as the English Sunday?' asked the young Frenchman François de La Rochefoucauld in 1784. These restrictions masked a historical anxiety about the presumed perils of having fun. If citizens chose to play bowls rather than practise their archery, the safety of the realm might be endangered. Games were a dangerous distraction.

During the nineteenth century people began to campaign for more freedom to enjoy themselves on Sundays and in 1855 the National Sunday League was established. This campaigned for more than forty years before Parliament agreed, in 1896, to open public museums and galleries on Sundays. Pressure continued in the twentieth century and the movement became the Brighter Sunday campaign. By the 1950s most English cinemas were showing films on Sunday but, in other parts of the UK, belief in the Sabbath still held sway. In Wales only one in ten cinemas would open and in Scotland it was one in twelve.

Sunday afternoon can be the best time to play quiet games with just a few people. These games have a calmer, slower pace. They take a little preparation but make a lovely alternative to snoring on the sofa in front of the football.

Hunt the Thimble

4 - 15

Medium

Thimble or matchbox

20 minutes

The word parlour comes from the Middle English word parlur, *which is itself a descendant of the Old French word* parleur *and the medieval Latin* parlatorium. *Originally the word referred to a room in a monastery or convent set aside for conversation. This was the place you would go for a chat with a member of your order or with someone from the outside world.*

The word also carries a suggestion of privacy, of a space set aside to be alone with someone. From the beginning the parlour was an intimate place. As the architecture of domestic housing changed and people started living in their own houses rather than in small huts, the word was used to describe the 'inner or more private room of a two roomed house, cottage or small farm'.

For the Victorians the parlour was somewhere to show off your stuff. The Victorians loved collecting things and they crammed their parlours with wax fruit, peacock feathers, ships in bottles, fans, photographs and stuffed animals. Trying to find a thimble in this treasure trove of trinkets and ornaments would have been much more challenging than scanning the minimalist interiors of today. But this game remains an enchanting challenge of ingenuity and awareness. It's made for a Sunday afternoon and if you are without a thimble a matchbox will do nicely.

Everyone leaves the room apart from one person. This person hides a thimble somewhere in the room. It should be difficult to discover but still in view. The rest of the company are called back in and must search for the thimble. Once players have spotted it they sit down. The search continues until one forlorn individual is left struggling to find an object which seems lost forever.

One thing I've learnt is to avoid sitting down too soon after seeing the thimble. Leave a short pause or you'll give the game away.

Kim's Game

Unlimited

Medium

Tray, cloth, pens and paper, lots of small objects

15 minutes

During the Renaissance, scholars used 'mind maps' to recall thousands of pieces of information. I have problems remembering my pin number. This game belongs to the mental gymnasium camp and I am sure I should play it more often. It's all about how you use the time you are given to peer at the objects. I'm convinced it's very good for you.

While everyone is out of the room take a tray and arrange on it twenty or thirty small objects and then cover it with a cloth. Call everyone back into the room and remove the cloth. Give everyone a minute to fix in their memory as many objects as possible. Then replace the cloth and give everyone five minutes to write the fullest list they can of the objects they have seen. The player with the longest and most accurate list wins.

Scents

Unlimited

Variable

Empty jam jars, strong smelling liquids, pens and cards

1 hour, preparation included

This game does take some time to prepare. It could either be the centre piece of a games night or something you idly put together late one Sunday morning to play with friends later that day. The pleasure lies in collecting the scents and finding the right balance between the dead easy and the downright impossible.

A large row of jam jars (you can tape paper around them to disguise the colour of the liquid) is placed on the table. Each of them has a number attached. At the bottom of each bottle is a small amount of liquid with a strong scent. You can use cooking liquids such as vinegar or vanilla essence, aromatic oils or more nefarious options like Dettol or bleach. A card with numbers corresponding to the bottles is given to each player and the game is to guess as many scents as possible.

Ping-Pong Donkey

4 - 20

Medium

Two table tennis bats, table tennis ball, large table

20 minutes

Ping-pong was invented by an engineer called James Gibbs as something to do when it rained. It was originally called Gossima and was played with balls made from champagne corks and bats from cigar box lids. It was renamed 'ping-pong' in 1901, after which it became a big hit. So, in acknowledgement of Gibbs' rainy day invention I share this with you. It's more riotous than other games in this section and it works well after Sunday lunch when everyone is a little tipsy. You don't need a table tennis table – a plain kitchen table with plenty of space to run round it will work fine.

You need two bats and a ball. Everyone stands around the table and as soon as someone has hit the ball the group rotates so that a different person returns the shot. The aim is to keep the rally going for as long as possible. It's easy to smash the ball to make a return impossible but more difficult to keep the shots low and regular. If you fail to pick up the bat, miss the ball or send it flying off the table then you get a letter. When your letters spell DONKEY, you go out. Once you get down to five players or below you are allowed to use your hand to bat the ball back. And when you are down to two, between every stroke you must complete a 360 degree turn.

Judge and Jury

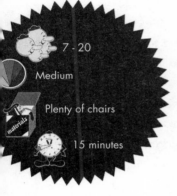

7 - 20

Medium

Plenty of chairs

15 minutes

Perhaps it has something to do with being English, but I have discovered that people love getting into lines and being shouted at. Once, faced with a crowd of uproarious ten-year-olds in a drama class in Northampton, I created a game called Drill. This involved me taking on the persona of a sergeant major and barking orders at the children to stand against the wall, run on the spot, scrub the floors, jump up and down etc. The only rule was that no one was allowed to laugh; if they did, they would be instantly disqualified. I must confess I took very readily to the role and, amazingly, so did the children. After an hour of endless messing about, they stood immediately to attention, determined to prove they could avoid cracking under pressure. Rather than teaching them the basics of voice and movement, I was forced to play this game with them for weeks afterwards. So, in the spirit of 'Northampton Drill' I share this game with you.

Players sit on chairs in two rows facing each other. Someone takes the role of judge and walks between the rows asking questions. When the judge questions someone, however, that person must not answer. The person sitting opposite them must speak instead, and without hesitation.

So the judge might ask one player, 'What is your favourite

colour?' That player must remain silent while the person opposite them must respond immediately, saying, for example, 'Red.' The answers don't have to be technically accurate or true; they just need to come from the right person at the right time. And there is a further catch. The words 'yes', 'no', 'black', 'white' and 'grey' are forbidden. So the judge needs to leap around trying to make the wrong person answer or prompt someone to say the forbidden words. As soon as a mistake is made, the person making the error becomes the new judge, but you can keep the same judge if someone is excelling in the part.

Up Jenkins!

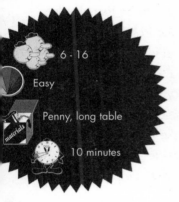

6 - 16

Easy

Penny, long table

10 minutes

For many years my dad worked as a publisher. He was known for making inspired but impulsive decisions. Inevitably, this meant that, after a few years of maverick triumphs, he would eventually come unstuck and get the sack.

Dad's last office was in Bedford Square. Sure enough, after a series of glittering but unorthodox decisions, the fateful call eventually arrived and I came home one day to discover Dad distraught. We all went with him in a white van to clear out his office. His desk was a long and ancient looking table. As no one seemed to want it, we loaded it into the van and drove home. There were some collective nerves about the table's value and so we were all sworn to secrecy about its origins. But it was never reclaimed and it proved very handy as both a dinner table and an essential prop for this game.

The game is a variant of the many that involve passing an object secretly between players, with another player trying to guess its whereabouts. A popular Victorian version was Hunt the Ring, where players passed a ring on a length of string around a circle, while trying to hide its progression from the player in the centre. Passing a slipper was another variant, this time with everyone sitting down and passing the slipper behind their backs. This game is another quick and easy version.

Two teams sit on opposite sides of the table. Placed on the table between the teams is a penny. One team closes their eyes, while the other takes the penny and starts to pass it between them, under the table. The other team now opens their eyes and one of them shouts, 'Up Jenkins!' The team hiding the coin must now raise their fists above their heads, still tightly clenched. The player who has made the call now carefully scans all the faces to see if she can spot the person who is clutching the coin. She should inspect the hands carefully to see if there is excessive redness from any unnatural squeezing.

This player can either now have a guess or try to discover some more information. If she chooses correctly at this stage, she wins three points. Otherwise she can call, 'Down Jenkins!' Now everyone must lower their fists onto the table and straighten out their hands, palms down. At this moment the caller can choose to make her second guess. If she is right, then she is awarded two points. If she is still not sure, however, she can call 'Open the Window!' This means that all the players must spread their fingers apart. At this point the coin is normally easy to spot. However, the niftiest player will find a way to slide the coin under his palm at a clever moment. If the caller guesses right, she is awarded one point and the teams reverse roles.

The first team to collect ten points is declared the winner.

Squails

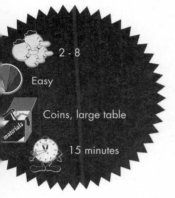

2 - 8

Easy

Coins, large table

15 minutes

In March 1936 The Times *published an article titled 'The Urgent Pursuit of Fun'. The article described various popular games of the day and ended with these lines: 'but of all the games of skill played by large parties at a table there has been nothing for excitement, for laughter, for thawing shyness, to come up to the old game of Squails, with its grotesque vocabulary, its hand-and-eye delighting implements, its call for skill ...' Despite its quality, by 1936 the game had fallen out of favour: '... the name of Squails is not to be found in every catalogue nowadays. If it has indeed dropped out of use, that is one more good reason for being truculently Victorian.'*

The word Squail comes from the Renaissance slang verb meaning to throw a loaded missile. The origins of the game itself are murky. Some historians have argued that the game is a precursor of shove-halfpenny; others argue that it was a Victorian invention. What we do know is that Squails was originally played using small metal discs around two centimetres in diameter and that each player was given three or four discs to play with. A small coin was placed in the middle of the table and a player's objective was to shoot a squail from the edge of the table, aiming at the coin in the centre and using the palm of the hand to 'shove' the coin in the desired direction. The winner was the player whose squail had come closest to the centre coin.

The Victorian version came with a customized set of equipment. It was played on a circular table with a raised boss in the centre, with a ring inscribed around it. The aim was, once again, to get as many discs inside the ring as possible, while knocking out the squails of other players.

So, if you want to get 'truculently Victorian' you can play this game on a table at home; a round or an oval one works best.

Place a small coin in the centre of the table. A penny is ideal. Give each player three coins each; these should be twice the size of the centre coin, so two pence coins are perfect. Each player shoots one of his coins in turn and is allowed to knock any squail – his own or another player's – out of position. He can also hit the centre coin. However, if he knocks this coin off the board he is eliminated from the game.

The winner is the player who has the nearest squail to the centre coin when all the squails have been shoved. In the early days of the game's history there were often rows about which squail had come closest and these conflicts had to be settled using a special measuring stick called a swoggle. Sadly, these exciting sounding objects are no longer available but a ruler will do the job just as well.

Shovelboard

2

Medium

Long table, two coins

15 minutes

Like Up Jenkins! this is another old game that needs a good sized flat surface. It was a favourite of Henry VIII's although I've discovered that a table tennis table works just as well as a medieval banqueting suite. It's good for Sunday afternoon as it takes little preparation and can be played by two players.

In the court of Henry VIII this game would have been played on a table about three feet wide and thirty feet long. But you can use a table tennis table with the net down. If you have access to a really long table then fantastic, otherwise the miniature version will do fine.

Two players stand at one end of the table. At the opposite end of the table, parallel to the edge and four or five inches back from it, draw a line. You can do this with chalk. Do the same, making another line, two feet back from the first. Each player then takes a ten pence piece. One by one players shove their pieces up the table. If the piece falls over the other edge then no score. No score either if the coin fails to make it past the first line. If it balances on the table's edge then good work – the player is awarded three points. If the coin stops between the farthest line and the edge, two points are awarded and if it comes to rest between the two lines, one point. Whoever reaches eleven points first, wins.

Jack Straws

2 - 10

Medium

Set of Jack Straws

15 minutes

The Chinese word for game is wan, a word that also means 'caressing a piece of jade to savour its smoothness' and 'the pleasure of a boat ride on a gentle lake or the prolonged contemplation of a waterfall'. Wow. Game playing in China, we discover, is linked to something tranquil, delicate and contemplative. Knowing this means it comes as less of a surprise that Jack Straws (Four-Five-Six, Spillicans or Pickup Sticks) originated in the Far East. The original sets were ornately carved collections of sticks made of ivory, with their ends sculpted into elaborate shapes – such as a trident, a bird on a branch or a horse's head. The more elaborate the shape, the harder it was to extract the stick from the pile and the more points each player earned.

Most people buy Jack Straws in kits. However, after explaining the rules I have included some instructions about how to make your own version of the game. On the whole I prefer games that are easy and quick and require minimum preparation time. But making your own set of Jack Straws is such an enjoyable and straightforward business that I've included instructions below.

Jack Straws is built around the idea of trying to extract differently coloured straws from the pile without causing any of the others to move. The value of the straws varies according to their colour. A typical scoring system would be as follows:

Blue	3 points
Red	5 points
Yellow	10 points
Green	15 points
Red and white	20 points

Everyone gathers around a table and one player is chosen to begin the game by dropping the sticks. First, that player mixes the straws thoroughly, bunches them in one hand and then, with the bottoms just touching the table, allows them to fall in a higgledy-piggledy, chaotic pile. Another player then starts. This player must use his hands to remove one stick after another, without causing any others to move or even tremble. Once he tries to move another stick he may not change his mind if this stick proves too hard. Once the player disturbs another stick, his turn is over and another player has a go.

Red and white sticks are valuable as, once these have been rescued, players may use them to retrieve other sticks which are too delicately positioned to be lifted by fingers alone. Another good trick is to exert pressure on one end of a stick to cause the other end to rise; you can then pivot the stick to safety. Once all the sticks have been collected, tally up the scores and the game is done.

Making Your Own Jack Straws

This is not a ten-minute job. However, you will feel enormous pride at the end of the process and you will have your very own custom-made game, which you can either give to someone as a present or pass down as a games heirloom.

The first thing you need to do is to get the wood. You are going to need fifty ten-inch lengths of wooden dowel with a diameter of around four millimetres. For this you need to find a friendly hardware store, with a friendly hardware store manager who will saw the dowel down into the lengths you need.

Once you've got your straws use a pencil sharpener to taper both ends. This is the arduous part. It will take you a few hours and you might want to enlist some team-mates to give you a hand if fatigue sets in.

Once all the straws have nice sharp ends, begin painting the straws different colours. The best way to do this is to buy some tester pots of emulsion paint and varnish from a big DIY shop, or you might have some old gloss paints lying around in a garage or shed. Following the scoring system explained above, paint twenty sticks blue, ten red, five yellow, three green and two with red and white stripes. If you want to be really fancy you make these stripes spiral along the straw like those poles hanging outside barber's shops.

Leave the straws to dry and then get spilling!

Code Breaker

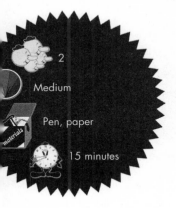

2

Medium

Pen, paper

15 minutes

You can buy this game in the shops under the title Mastermind. The game comes with plastic pegs and a tray, but you can just as easily play it using a pen and paper.

This is a game for two people. The first player comes up with a code featuring a sequence of four single-digit numbers. In the code all four numbers have to be different, for example 2, 4, 6, 8. The job of the other player is to work out the code by making a series of guesses.

The first player writes his code at the top of a piece of paper and covers it. Underneath the second player writes his first guess, for example 1, 4, 8, 5.

The first player places a tick above the numbers that are correct and in the right place – so the 4 gets a tick. He places a dot above numbers that are correct but in the wrong position, so a dot would go above the 8, and a cross above the numbers that don't feature at all – the 1 and the 5. The second player keeps submitting guesses down the page until he eventually earns four ticks and the code at the top of the page is revealed.

The aim of the game is to crack the code with the smallest number of guesses. So when this round is over, you swap roles to see if the other player can do any better. After two rounds, the winning player is awarded a point and you can play another match. You can make the game more difficult by allowing numbers to be repeated or by extending the length of the code.

Victorian Yoga

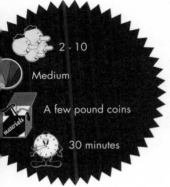

2 - 10

Medium

A few pound coins

30 minutes

These unusual acrobatic games and 'feats' date back centuries. They take a little bit of figuring out but it's worth it; no yoga mats required.

One person lies flat on the floor, then is lifted by another into an upright position by a pair of hands under the back of his head as he keeps rigid at all times.

Keeping your feet behind a line, see who can stretch along the ground, supported by their left hand only, to place a pound coin with their right hand the furthest distance away. Each player must then return to an upright position again, behind the line, without moving their feet or using their right hand for support. When you've done this, you must recover the pound coin in the same way. Whoever makes it back with no faults wins all the coins.

Keeping your feet together and your left arm beside you, see how far back from a wall you can place your feet (remembering that you have to get into an upright position again) while you lean forward, supported by your right hand laid flat against the wall. No prizes for falling over.

And here is an Impossible Feat. Standing a person against the wall with his heels touching it, lay a pound coin a foot or so in front of him, and tell him it will be his if he can pick it up without moving his heels from the wall. Your pound is safe.

Games for a Long Journey

A couple of weeks before my thirtieth birthday I got dumped. I had left my job in Northampton to become a student again, studying physical theatre at a new school in Ladbroke Grove. It was the summer break and I had nothing to do, no money and no girlfriend. I needed an adventure. And so I decided to embrace the cliché: to cash in my savings and make a trip to India.

My plan was to begin in the north of the country and make my way south by train. A family friend I met in Delhi warned me of the dangers of train travel and insisted that I buy a padlock to make sure no one stole my luggage as I slept. So, armed with a rather feeble looking chain and padlock I boarded the Kerala Express from Delhi to Ernakulam: total travelling time? Three days.

I spent the first few hours with a retired general and a middle-aged stationmaster who was keen to explain that, as an employee of the railways, he was able to travel anywhere in India free of charge. The general, meanwhile, was anxious to know about the cost of living in London, whether girls smoked and 'took liquor' and why I wasn't married. When he got off, the stationmaster started expounding the values of yoga, demonstrating the lotus position and alternate nostril breathing. This was clearly going to be an unusual journey.

At Bhopal the stationmaster got off and I was joined by two new companions. One was a middle-aged woman called Jaya, who worked as a GP in Bhopal and spoke excellent English. The other was a man named Bharadwaj, a gentle, shy man with only broken English. Both were travelling to Kerala to visit their respective families. The compartment we shared was not large and we began by hiding politely behind our books. Then, in the way that is common in India among strangers, conversation began. I explained that I had come away for an adventure after breaking up with my girlfriend and Jaya spoke about her own travels in Europe and her work running a school for street children in Bhopal. The three of us began to relax and, as the evening approached, I decided to tell my new friends that tomorrow was my birthday.

The next morning, as young men ran along the corridors crying, 'Chai! Chai!', I was woken by a gentle tapping on the shoulder. In a little pile in front of me lay a birthday card, an apple and a book entitled *Where Is God When It Hurts?* Jaya had made the card during the night, Bharadwaj had donated the apple and the book was

Jaya's reading for the journey, but she felt that my need was greater. Surprised, delighted and touched, I wriggled out of my sleeping bag, folded back my upper-berth bunk and sat down for a chai and rice breakfast.

And so began one of the strangest and most magical birthdays of my life. As we swept across the Indian countryside the three of us played I-Spy, Twenty Questions and Scissors, Paper and Stone. In a railway carriage, with endless hours before us and nothing in common but our status as travellers, games became our sustenance. As the Indian countryside flashed by, these games bound us together in an unrepeatable, life-affirming world of our own making.

The train journey was a sign of things to come. After arriving in Kerala, Jaya put me in touch with a local school outside Cochin, where I taught drama in exchange for somewhere to stay and meals in the school canteen. While there, I was introduced to Alex M. Matthew, an Indian man in his late fifties, who was the school bursar. Over lunch in the school canteen on my first day he introduced himself and presented me with his card, which proudly declared his expertise in:

TAXATION, BUSINESS, HUMAN RESOURCE, MANAGEMENT, FINANCE AND INDUSTRY.

He also taught yoga. Clearly a man of many talents, Alex and I became friends and he offered to teach me the basics of yoga in the early mornings. So I would stagger out of bed at six thirty every morning to meet him on a terrace overlooking the city to work through our camel, dolphin and tree poses. He was a gentle man and after our classes we would chat about our lives. I gradually began to share my passion for games and Alex began to share the bits and bobs he knew. He explained how the English game Snakes and Ladders had grown out of a famous Indian game called Jnana Chaupar, which was translated as the 'game of knowledge'. In Jnana the aim was to reach 'karmic bliss'. If you landed on a virtue, you would climb a ladder to reach the god Vishnu and if you landed on a vice – an obstacle of karma – you were swallowed by a snake and would have to retreat several spaces. On my return to England I discovered that he was absolutely right. The game was first repackaged and sold in Britain in 1892.

Not all journeys are as epic as the one I enjoyed in India. But driving to school every morning, travelling on trains to work or being stuck for hours in airports are all scenarios that can be enlivened by games. You may not find your companions quite as amenable as my fellow train passengers, but you'll be amazed at how infectious game playing can be.

 Games for a Long Journey

Ink Pink

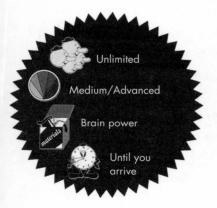

Unlimited

Medium/Advanced

Brain power

Until you arrive

I was once in a car driving from London to Chichester to see a matinee. The traffic was terrible so someone suggested this game. We arrived at the theatre to hear the sound of applause. We stayed for a cup of tea before heading back home. After a round trip of nearly six hours in the car, we arrived back in London strangely euphoric. The play had been missed but a great new game had been learnt.

Someone thinks of two words which rhyme and which both have the same number of syllables, for example 'Hell, Bell'. This player then provides two clues to help people guess the words. The first clue refers to the number of syllables. So, for 'Hell, Bell' the player would begin by saying, 'Ink, Pink', because this is the clue that is always used to mean that both words have only one syllable each. The second clue refers to the meaning of the words. In this example the player might say, 'Infernal, Chime'. For each clue you are only allowed to give two words. Others now have to guess what the words might be.

For pairs of words with two syllables (like 'Gentle Lentil' or 'Jelly Belly') you would introduce them by saying 'Inky Pinky', before giving your second clue. For words of three syllables (and now you get really crazy) like 'Towaway Stowaway' or 'Floataway Motorway' you say 'Inkity Pinkity' before giving your cryptic clue.

You quickly enter the world of Lewis Carroll but this is part of the fun. As you get better at the game the aim becomes to think of longer pairs of words which both rhyme and which share the same number of syllables.

Ghosts

2 - 8

Medium

A fierce determination to win

30 minutes

When I worked at the theatre in Northampton, part of my job involved driving round the country seeing productions with my boss, Rupert Goold, who is now directing shows in the West End. He taught me this game on a car journey to Leeds. He was enormously competitive and refused to lose a single round. This meant agonizing silences while he plotted his next move. If you can win at this game, it bodes well.

Someone proposes a letter from the alphabet. Any will do. Let's take 'A'. The person next to them – going clockwise – must add another letter before or after the 'A' *without making a word.*

So, if you added 'S' after the 'A' you would make 'AS', which is something you want to avoid. However, if you were to put the 'S' before the 'A' then no problem – you would have 'SA' – and the spotlight turns to the next player. He or she must add another letter, either at the beginning or end of the sequence, always trying to avoid making a word.

Players must always have a word in mind. Letters cannot be added randomly. If a player suspects this he can 'bluff'

the player before him, demanding that the player reveal the word he had in mind. If he can't answer that player loses a life and a new chain begins. However, if this player *does* have a word then the player who called his bluff loses a life.

It's called Ghosts because you have three lives. With your first error you become a 'third of a ghost', with your second error 'two thirds of a ghost' and then, finally, a 'whole ghost' and out of the game you go.

Another addict of this game was the American writer James Thurber. Don't play it too often or you might start displaying some of the symptoms he describes below:

> I sometimes keep on playing the game, all by myself, after it is over and I have gone to bed. On a recent night, tossing and spelling, I spent two hours hunting for another word besides phlox that has 'hlo' in it. I finally found seven: 'matchlock', 'decathlon', 'pentathlon', 'hydrochloric', 'chlorine', 'chloroform', and 'monthlong'. There are more than a dozen others, but I had to look them up in the dictionary the next day, and that doesn't count.

> Starting words in the middle and spelling them in both directions lifts Ghosts out of the realm of

children's parties and ladies sewing circles and makes it into a game to test the mettle of the mature adult mind. The Ghost aficionado is a moody fellow, given to spelling to himself at the table, not listening to his wife and staring at his frightened children, wondering why he didn't detect, in yesterday's game that 'cklu' is the guts of 'lacklustre' and priding himself on having stumped everyone with 'nehe', the middle of 'swineherd'.

Fortunately, Unfortunately

As many as you like

Extremely easy

Nothing

There is no end!

This is a fun game for the car and it's a nice twist on the game where you create a story in a group, each one of you saying one word at a time. In this game the story can become so surreal so quickly that it's often hard to find the stamina to keep going. This version, however, manages to balance inventiveness with structure. It's so simple that as soon as I describe it to anyone I immediately find myself playing it. You can play it with any number of players but an odd number is best as you get to change who says which phrase ...

Someone begins a story by volunteering an opening sentence such as 'I arrived in Berlin as the snow began to fall'. The next player replies by saying a sentence beginning with 'Fortunately', so they might say 'Fortunately I knew the city well'. The next player must begin his next sentence with 'Unfortunately' so they might reply 'Unfortunately I had recently lost my memory'. This might be followed with 'Fortunately I discovered a map in my pocket' and that by 'Unfortunately it was a map of New York', and so on. The game continues with players alternating sentences until you arrive at your destination, the story reaches its natural end or you just can't stand it anymore.

Why Did I Say That?

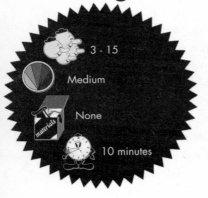

3 - 15

Medium

None

10 minutes

This is a memory game with a twist. There is something satisfying about not having to remember the word you said but, rather, the word that made you say it. It's a game that Victorians would have played warming themselves by the fire but it works equally well on a long car journey.

Everyone sits near each other. You might be in the car, around a table on a train, or sitting together at home. Someone begins by saying an object, for example, 'Rose'. The next player says a word that 'Rose' makes them think of: 'Hip', for example. This process continues round the circle with everyone saying associated words, so you might get 'Rose – Hip – Trendy – Nightclub – Bouncer'. Keep going for seven rounds or so until you have gathered plenty of links in the chain. Then try and retrace your steps all the way back to your first word, in this case 'Rose'.

And here is the catch. Rather than remembering your own word you have to remember the word that came before yours. So the player who said 'Bouncer' would say, in this reverse journey, 'Nightclub'. The player who previously said 'Nightclub' would say 'Trendy', and so on. Everyone must remember and say the word that went before their own.

The game takes concentration but it's an ecstatic moment when you finally find your way home.

Roadside Whist

As many as can fit in your car

Easy

Changing views

materials

The length of your journey

This game apparently originated in the Channel Islands, where visitors riding around in large open wagons would enjoy the holidays playing Roadside Whist. If you don't have a wagon it's equally good played in the car.

People sitting in the left side of the car take the left side of the road and those on the right, the right. The game is organized on a scoring system explained by the 'Conductor' at the beginning of the game. I have come up with a potential score list, but it's just a start to help you to create your own.

On the journey, if you see:

A Mini	you score	1
A Church	you score	2
A Postman	you score	3
A Field of Sheep	you score	4
A Ladder against a House	you score	5

An Open Gate	you score	6
A Field of Rabbits	you score	7
A Soldier	you score	8
A White Horse	you score	9
A Cat on a Window Ledge	you score	10

The team with the greatest number of points at the end of the journey wins.

Crambo

2 - 15

Medium

Just players

10 minutes

In 1660 Samuel Pepys set out on a voyage to The Hague. He was accompanying his boss, benefactor and patron, Edward Montagu. Their aim was to return home with the king. This was the period just after the death of Oliver Cromwell when the government was in a state of near collapse. Many of the nobles who had advocated the death of Charles I were reversing their position and campaigning for the restoration of the monarchy. Montagu was one of these and he was now leading the mission to bring back Charles II from exile in Holland.

Pepys gives us a vivid account of how he spent his time during the crossing. Rather than playing fruit machines and eating bad croissants, Pepys played his violin, 'walked upon the deck to keep myself from being sick', played nine pins and watched pretty girls on a passing boat through a friend's telescope. On arriving in Holland, while Montagu got on with the business of negotiating with the king, Pepys rode about in his carriage visiting sites and buying gifts for his family. He also played games. In his diary he records this tantalizing entry: 'again play at Crambo in the wagon, Mr Edward, Mr Ibbot, Mr Pinney and I'.

Here we have one of the earliest mentions in literature of playing games on a journey. It's frustratingly brief. From the 'again' we can deduce that this was a game Pepys and his companions played a lot. And I'm not surprised since it's a really good one.

Even the Oxford English Dictionary acknowledges that the roots of the word Crambo are unclear. It suggests that it might come from 'crambe', which refers to a particular kind of regurgitated cabbage. This definition suggests something that is repeated in an unwelcome way. Certainly the game involves having various attempts at guessing a word but I can promise you it's much more fun than anything that involves cabbage – regurgitated or otherwise.

You can play this in a group or in pairs. (I've even played it to revive a particularly slow-moving Valentine's night dinner; so it's a good one to have up your sleeve.)

With one player out of earshot everyone else chooses a word. When the player comes back in she is told a word that rhymes with the word that has been chosen. Let's say that the word chosen is **night**; this means the clue you might be given might be **light**. Now the player has to ask questions of everyone without saying the word itself. She has to ask indirect questions in the style of the examples given below:

Guesser: Is it the opposite of wrong?

Player: No, it is not **right**.

Guesser: Is it one of the five senses?

Player: No, it is not **sight**.

Guesser: Is it the colour of flour?

Player: No, it is not **white**.

And so on, until the word is guessed successfully. The fun here is that everyone has to be creative. The guesser has to frame questions inventively and the other players have to work out the word that the guesser is referring to.

There are some good variations of this game. If you really hit your stride you can play Rhyming Crambo. Once more, someone thinks of a word and provides a word it rhymes with. The other players have to think of a potential word and then frame their questions in a rhyming couplet. This is how it might work:

Clue: **Stamp**

Q: I might use it instead of the stair
       Especially if I am in a wheelchair.

A: It is not **ramp**.

Q: I've got no clothes, I've got no house
       I live on the street, just like a mouse.

A: It is not **tramp**.

Q: Oh dear, oh dear, I'm all wet through,
      My brolly's broken, what shall I do?

A: It *is* **damp**.

And if you really want to top the Crambo heights, you can play Dumb Crambo. This is a game to play in a group and you need some space to move around. Someone thinks of a word and gives the rhyming clue as normal. The rest of the group then has to create a tableau communicating their suggestion. So, if they are given the clue '**rat**', the group might make the image of a group of extremely overweight people, to which the first player might say 'it is not **fat**'. They would follow this with another image, perhaps that of people wiping their feet, to which the first player might respond 'it is not **mat**'.

As always with Crambo, both sides need to be creative. Here the actors have to think of an idea and act it clearly, while the first player has the pleasure of trying to decode their images. The game continues until the word is eventually guessed.

The Harry Parkin Game

Unlimited

Advanced

Verbal dexterity

There is no end!

There is a category of game called 'backstage games'. During a run of shows, actors like playing long-running games and challenges. Being together with the same group every night for two months, or sometimes much longer, you need to find ways of staying on the ball, alleviating boredom and creating a convivial atmosphere. As these games are constantly interrupted by actors going on and coming off stage, they need to be flexible and loose and people need to be able to volunteer contributions if and when they can. One such game is the Harry Parkin Game.

As a freelance theatre director you travel wherever the work is. Like an actor, you are constantly moving around doing different kinds of plays in different kinds of spaces. One Christmas I found myself directing a musical version of A Christmas Carol at a fringe theatre in west London. The theatre wasn't subsidized and only seated eighty people. With the best possible box office predictions, the theatre couldn't afford to employ more than four actors. So, over three weeks' rehearsal the actors and I set about adapting the story, trying to find as many ingenious tricks and effects as we could to pull off the story. Managing the box office, the publicity, the front of house, the props and script development was Harry Parkin, the general manager. This is a game he invented.

You can establish the rules at the beginning of a long car journey and

then let people come up with suggestions as the hours pass. Some
people can come up with ideas in seconds; others will take hours and
then deliver an absolute peach. One thing is for certain: the game will
keep nagging at you for days afterwards.

Someone begins by saying 'I've got a new job'. Everyone
else replies by saying, 'Oh, great, what are you doing?'
This person must reply by giving their new professional title
and a pun about their new position. For example:

I've got a new job.
Fantastic, what are you doing?
I'm a tea lady.
Great, how's it going?
*Good but I don't **earn** much!*

Or

I've got a new job.
Fantastic, what are you doing?
I'm a lift attendant.
How's it going?
Up and down.

Here are some more fine, very groanworthy examples:

I'm managing a walking stick shop.
How's it going?
*Nice shop, but you **can't get the staff**.*

I work for a diamond drilling company.
How's it going?
*Sounds glamorous, but it's really a **bit boring**.*

I'm a bin man.
How's it going?
Rubbish.

I'm an electrician.
How's it going?
*Good, but it's **hard to switch off**.*

Games on Trains

Trains ushered in new possibilities for games playing. Games like Crambo were good games to play in a stagecoach because you didn't see very much; you just had to be able to hear your partner's voice. Coaches were gloomy, with windows that were covered with oiled silks or other kinds of material to stop the rain coming through. The desire to keep out the elements was paramount and so windows were also kept as small as possible. This meant travelling in a state of near darkness. However, in 1830 the first scheduled passenger train set off and travelling conditions changed.

The popularity of trains spread fast. During 1842 just over twenty-four million passengers travelled by train, and by 1846 the number had soared to nearly forty-four million. Commenting on the thousands of people leaving Manchester on the excursion train at Whitsuntide in 1845, the *Manchester Guardian* wrote 'the birth of this new and cheap means of transit is as if the wings of the wind have been given for a week to the closely confined operative, the hard working mechanic and the counter riveted shopkeeper. They enjoy the needful relaxation from the toil or care or confinement of business; they see new scenes and acquire new tastes for the beautiful in nature.' It was this same year that a young temperance worker, Thomas Cook, had the idea of devoting himself full time to organizing railway excursions. These train journeys were eventually to make him very famous indeed.

Compartments in the new trains were much better lit than the stagecoaches of old; oil and, later, gas lamps now made reading possible. The publisher George Newnes was one of the first men to realize the potential of trains as places where you could do more than just look out of the window. In 1881 he began publishing *Tit Bits*, a hugely popular amalgam of strange facts, new stories, jokes and riddles. The success of this magazine led to Alfred Harmsworth establishing the *Daily Mail* in 1896. It cost half a penny and for the first time substantial numbers of working people began reading a daily paper.

It took time for people to come round to playing games on trains. One of the earliest references that we have comes from Lewis Carroll.

Lewis Carroll was games mad. As a child he built elaborate replica stations in his garden and through his life created a plethora of word games, puzzles and magic tricks. He was particularly fond of drawings which played tricks on the viewer. In one well-known example he drew a picture story about a husband and wife who lived in a house by a lake. Carroll would end his explanation of his picture with the wife declaring, 'My dear, you are a perfect goose.' When he had finished telling the story and drawing the picture, he would turn the picture of an idyllic lakeside scene upside down to reveal the Perfect Goose.

We have a great account of how seriously Carroll took games playing on long journeys. Writing in the *Strand* magazine just after his death in 1898, his friend Beatrice Hatch remembered:

> If he took you up to London to see a play you were no sooner seated in your railway carriage than a game was produced from his bag and all the occupants of the compartment were invited to join in playing a kind of 'halma' or 'draughts' of his own invention, on the little wooden board that had specially been made at his design for railway use, with 'men' warranted not to tumble down, because they fitted into little holes in the board!

So in the spirit of Lewis Carroll, here are some ideas to get you going.

Guggenheim

This game has a slow rhythm and is ideal for a long train journey. It needs time for people to gather their thoughts and the pleasure lies as much in others' suggestions as your own. When you have completed the game it's fun to mark each other's papers to heighten the feeling of a shared activity as well as to prevent any cheating!

3 - 10

Medium

Pens and paper

30 minutes

P. G. Wodehouse was a fan of this game, otherwise known as Categories. He apparently supplied this name after being inspired by the many objects in the Guggenheim Museum in New York.

Hand round pens and paper. Everyone agrees five general categories with plenty of examples; for instance plays, animals, cities, puddings or musical instruments. Everyone writes these categories down in a vertical column on the left-hand side of their papers.

Together choose a word of five or six letters. It's good to avoid words where letters are repeated so 'Horse' is better than 'Spoon'. Everyone writes the agreed word across the top of their papers. Then give people ten or fifteen minutes to fill in the grid by giving examples of the category on the left beginning with each different letter of the word above.

For example, if the word along the top is 'Horse' and the first category on the left was 'Cities' then you would write under 'H' a city beginning with 'H', Honolulu perhaps. You'd then write a second city beginning with 'O' under the 'O' and then another beginning with 'R'. Once you've written a city under each letter you go down to the next line and complete the next category. The grid is complete when you have filled in all the gaps.

Scoring comes next. If you have a blank – i.e. if you couldn't think of an example for that square – then you have one point deducted (this encourages people to try). If you have a word which someone else in the circle has too, that example is crossed out and you don't receive any points. If you have a word which no one else has thought of, then you score a point. So you are searching for examples that are as unusual as possible. Not as easy as it seems.

Trailers

2 - 10

Medium

Pen and paper

15 minutes

This is another pen and pencil game that is much simpler and shorter than Guggenheim. It's one of many games you can play around acronyms.

Take a film title and write it down one side of the paper in a vertical column. Then ask everyone to write a slogan that describes the film, using each letter to make a word. For example, for *Jaws*, you might write 'Jaw-dropping, atmospheric, water story'. Can you do better? I suspect you can. You can award points for the best slogan in each round, but I think it works best as a doodle game – an amusing way to pass the time on the train, between looking out of the window and falling asleep.

Wiggle-Waggle

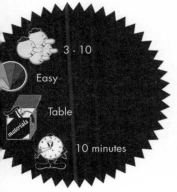

3 - 10

Easy

Table

10 minutes

This game is good to play when you are sitting in the airport café, when you've finished your lunch with still a good hour or so before take-off. It's a version of Simon Says and it's a good way to keep your spirits up as you wait for the departure board to usher you onwards.

Players sit around a table. A leader is appointed who is called Buck. Everyone has their fingers clenched into a fist and their thumbs extended. When Buck says 'Thumbs up', everyone places both fists on the table with their thumbs sticking up straight. When Buck says 'Thumbs down', the position is reversed; people rest their thumbs on the table with their fists pointing into the air. When Buck says 'Hands flat', people lay their hands flat on the table. Finally, when Buck says 'Wiggle-waggle', people move their hands between the thumbs-down and the thumbs-up position, performing a kind of wiggle-waggle dance movement.

But players must only adopt these postures when the instructions are preceded by 'Buck says …' When giving the false call, i.e. by missing out 'Buck says ...', the leader can still do the movement, for example saying 'Hands down' while laying his own hands flat on the table. The leader can also cause gleeful confusion by performing the opposite movement of the words being said, for example laying his hands flat on the table while saying 'Buck says, thumbs up'.

The game becomes an amazing assault on people's hand/eye coordination skills.

Squiggle

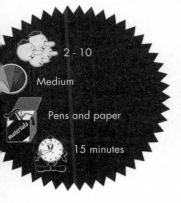

2 - 10

Medium

Pens and paper

15 minutes

Freud believed that the value of games lay in their potential for relieving tension. Games help you to relax. He also argued that they were forms of wish fulfilment. In the imaginary world of the game you could take action, manipulate reality, win over the odds. As Freud developed his work into the unconscious he also became curious about ways to discover what was really going on in the hidden depths of the psyche. Involuntary slips, jokes, dreams, all became fascinating signs, pointing to the workings of a secret self.

Games have been used by psycho-analysts ever since. Drawing games are often used to allow patients, especially children, to free-associate and to share thoughts more easily expressed through images than words.

This game works well on a train journey, where you have tables to lean on and you have plenty of time to enjoy the drawing part. You can happily play it with two people or more. With more players, the stakes rise; however, I feel the game works best without too much pressure being applied.

Each player is given a sheet of paper. A4 size is fine. Each player needs a different coloured felt-tip pen or a pencil. The game begins by players making five abstract squiggles on their papers. They should have plenty of space around them and not be too large. The more abstract the better. Players now exchange their pieces of paper and a time limit is set. I would suggest between two and five minutes depending on how many players you have and how long your journey is. During this time players must use all the five squiggles to create five separate pictures. Inventiveness is more important here than artistic expertise. There is something very nice about gently transforming a squiggle into a picture and people tend to enjoy being given the chance to create something satisfying.

Of course, there is no objective way of judging art, especially squiggle art. However, once the time is up and people show their finished works, a winner will undoubtedly emerge.

The Key of the King's Garden

2 - 20

Medium

Good memories

15 minutes

Games can appear in unlikely places. I found this one in the Plymouth and Cornish Advertiser dated 20 December 1882. It's a variation of those games where you have to remember long lists of objects. This version requires imagination as well as a good memory. You could play it at Christmas with everyone collapsed after the turkey. But, since you don't need any materials (other than a good memory), it's a good game to play while waiting for your delayed flight.

With everyone sitting around a table or in a circle, a player starts by saying, 'I give you the key of the king's garden'. The next player responds by adding another stage to the beginning of the original sentence. She might respond by saying, 'I give you the string that holds the key of the king's garden'. This might be followed by the next player saying, 'I give you the scissors to cut the string that holds the key of the king's garden', followed by 'I give you a file to sharpen the scissors to cut the string to hold the key of the king's garden', followed by 'I give you a box in which to keep the file to sharpen the scissors to cut the string to hold the key of the king's garden'. You keep going until a player stumbles, who then goes out. Keep going until there is just one player left standing.

Hands Down

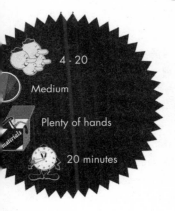

4 - 20

Medium

Plenty of hands

20 minutes

Everyone sits or kneels in a circle. Everyone puts both palms flat on the floor in front of them, so that they form a circle of hands. Now everyone lifts their right palm off the ground and places it on the ground on the other side of the person on their right's left palm. This means that between your palms lies someone else's. To achieve this you have to squeeze up close to each other as everyone's palms must be flat on the ground for the game to work.

Now someone starts by tapping the ground with one hand. Going clockwise, the next player taps his hand on the ground and you keep going in this same direction. However, at any point a player may make a double tap, which means the direction of the tapping now changes to go anti-clockwise. A double tap can be met with another double tap, so the tapping can constantly change direction if the players wish it. Because, in between your palms, lies another's, these changes of direction will be surprisingly hard to manage. The rhythm is fast and if there are any pauses or if a hand comes up off the floor out of sequence, then that hand must be removed from the sequence. When both hands are eliminated their owner leaves the game. As this happens, keep locking arms as much as possible to keep a hand between your own.

You can play with lots of players and it's a fantastic test of attention and coordination.

The Imaginary Family

2 - 7

Easy

Just imagination

As long as you can keep the story going

Lots of games involve mimicry. They are about creating a parallel universe. We only need to remember playing with toy soldiers or dolls to be reminded of how early in life we start to enjoy making up stories. Eventually worlds conjured up by a group of people playing together become something we pay to see in a theatre. We go to watch people playing. This is a game to be played last thing at night, instead of a bedtime story. I don't have any kids but I hope that, when I do, I will play this game with them.

Begin by creating your family. How many people are there? How old are the children? What are their names? Does the family have a pet? Then everyone tells the story of what happens to the family. Where do they go? What adventures do they have? What discoveries do they make? Every day of your holiday you can create another episode in their journey. Everyone becomes linked as you climb a ladder together into imaginary worlds.

SEASONAL SPECIALS

Seasonal Specials

Rural Games in Dorset

Marilyn Fox was a director at the BBC. When I first met her she had just directed the BBC adaptation of *The Lion, the Witch and the Wardrobe*. I was thirteen, desperate to act and had just started classes at the Anna Scher Theatre School in Islington. Marilyn was looking to cast her new series for BBC1, an adaptation of *Five Children and It* by E. Nesbit. Anna Scher was known mainly for training young inner-city actors for shows like *Grange Hill*, but Marilyn was keen to explore all avenues and so decided to pay the school a visit one Friday evening.

Travelling down from St Albans every week and with a plummy middle-class accent, I couldn't help but stand out. At the end of the class, Marilyn asked me to come upstairs to the office and read some of the script. I didn't really understand what the project was, or the title, which just seemed plain odd. But I did my best to say lines like 'Not so dusty!' with as much gusto as I could and some weeks later the BBC rang and asked me to go for a recall at Television Centre. Weeks and many more auditions later, I was finally offered the part of Cyril, nickname Squirrel, the eldest of the five children.

Five Children and It tells the story of five children who together discover a magical creature called a Psammead who lives in a sandpit and grants children wishes. The children wish for all the things you would expect – wings, gold, beauty – and the story reveals how these wishes backfire every time, with the children being marooned on the top of a church tower, left in a ditch, and, finally, arrested by the local police. Sensible children, the book teaches, wish for sensible things.

And so I was whisked out of school and into a world of Victorian period drama: horse-drawn carriages, tweed caps, maids and country houses. The four other children and I stayed for two months in the Wessex Royale, a small hotel in Dorchester. As well as an entrée into a make-believe Victorian world, this was also a thrilling way into the world of *grown-ups*. I was fascinated by the actors who passed through the Royale – coachmen, coppers, maids and vicars – each of whom would have beguiling anecdotes about working with celebrities. My official drink was lime and soda but occasionally they would buy me the odd Baileys or even, one special night, my first Jack Daniel's. My excitement at being around adults continued on the set where I was distracted from learning my lines by my ham-fisted attempts to seduce the make-up ladies.

In the evenings after a day's filming, the crew would make

trips to local pubs and occasionally the children were allowed to join them. Many of these rural Dorset pubs still had traditional skittle alleys. We would join in with the adults playing this long established game, which has been part of our games culture for centuries. Being in Dorset over these long summer months gave me an insight into games that are played at certain times of the year and are connected to the rural calendar.

We don't have many games that still link us intimately to specific periods of time, but increasingly we want to celebrate the passing of the seasons. Over the last few years I have been researching this forgotten games calendar. Perhaps this interest harks back to a life marked out and remembered through rituals. Certainly games once performed this function. So in this chapter I want to share with you a mixture of familiar games and more archaic ones, to help you celebrate the pleasures of the changing year.

Beach Games in Summer

There are two types of beaches in the UK: the wild and the sedate. In Cornwall the waves are rough, dogs run up and down, people fly kites and your ice cream melts by the time you've made it from the ice-cream van to your towel. In Suffolk people drink tea on the beach and play Scrabble. In Cornwall people play cricket on the beach; in Suffolk they read about it in the *Observer*. I enjoy both kinds of beaches equally but, for the games player, the wild beach wins hands down. For these games you need space to run.

Pebbles

6 - 30

Easy

10 pebbles

5 minutes

'There is one joy of childhood, however, that one can never recapture, and that is the joy of getting wet in the sea,' wrote A. A. Milne. Certainly the first game everyone plays on the beach is running by the waves trying to avoid getting your feet wet. However, as Milne implies, this is a game which wilts over time. So here is a simple, nimble game you can play with your family and friends as easily as you did when you first fled the unpredictable reach of the waves.

Players stand in two rows facing each other. The top one in each row holds five pebbles in his hand. The game is to see which row can most quickly pass all the pebbles down to the bottom of the row and back up again. Each player must take each pebble first in one hand, then in the other and then pass it on to the next player and never have two pebbles travelling in the same direction in one hand at the same time.

Kingy

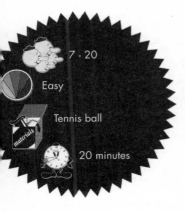

7 - 20

Easy

Tennis ball

20 minutes

During the fifties and sixties, when the famous games researchers Iona and Peter Opie were carrying out their massive survey of the games being played in the streets and playgrounds of Britain, one of the most popular games they discovered was Kingy. Unlike many of the games they found, whose rules varied widely in different parts of the country, this game was not only universally known but was played with remarkable consistency. So it's striking that, by the late seventies and early eighties, it had largely faded from view. The Opies' careful description has helped me play it for the first time and I can recommend reviving it.

This is a good game for the beach since you can dive around to dodge the ball without any fear of falling on a hard surface. You do need to define your playing space by marking out the four corners with jumpers or towels, and do make sure you set up your area some way away from sunbathers, who might not welcome being roused by a stray tennis ball in their teacup.

Someone is ON. She has the tennis ball and stands in the middle of your playing area. She must keep still and try to throw the ball at one of the other players, who are allowed to keep moving. Once someone is hit, he or she joins the player who is ON. Those players who are ON throw the ball to each other and then run to a new position, trying all the time to hit the other players, who, once hit, must then join them. The key point is that if you are holding the ball you can't move. The game continues until everyone has been hit and there is one player left who is declared the King.

Once you establish the basic rules, you can allow players being hunted to fist the ball away. (In Lancashire the game was traditionally known as Dustbin as players were allowed to fend off the ball with bats, pieces of wood and even dustbin lids – kind of *Test Match Special* meets *Stomp*.) Contact with any other part of the players' bodies is, however, forbidden, and if this happens they must join the throwers. The aim is for the game to become fast and fluid. The players throwing the ball need to work together to pass the ball smoothly between each other before making a successful strike.

There is a traditional way of deciding who is ON at the beginning of the game. Everyone stands in a circle with their hands clenched into fists in front of them. One player throws the ball to someone else who must catch it in their fists. They, in turn, throw it to someone else until the first player who drops it becomes ON. As they reach down to pick the ball up, everyone else runs off and the game begins.

Flip-Flop

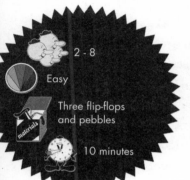

2 - 8

Easy

Three flip-flops and pebbles

10 minutes

The pleasure of knocking things down seems ingrained in the human experience. The Opies recorded this interview with a nine-year-old from East Finchley in the 1960s, who explained that his 'very best game outside is called Knock It Down. You stand five tins on top of each other and in your hand you have two tennis balls. You take aim carefully and fire one tennis ball. And it is smashing fun.'

Knocking things over goes way back. Loggats was an old game played at fairs. The game involved throwing club-like sticks at a post. The game was also popular at sheep shearing festivals where the prize was a black fleece, presented to the winner by the farmer's maidservant. Loggats was a sibling of the Aunt Sally games. The word sally derives from the French *saillir*, meaning to stick out. The game was traditionally constructed around a pole with a platform on the top, on which was balanced a 'dolly', which was simply a piece of wood. The aim of the game was to knock the dolly from the platform. Here is my version for the beach.

Take three flip-flops and stick them into the sand. Make sure they are in firmly but still have plenty of flip-flop showing. Ask everyone playing to collect five pebbles each and then establish a throwing line a couple of metres away from the shoes. One by one, players should stand behind the line (a towel is a good thing to use here) and throw their five pebbles, being awarded one point for every successful hit. Keep going over several rounds, establishing twenty points as the target. The first player to reach this score wins and gets to sunbathe in peace while the loser has to perform a forfeit, such as buying everyone ice creams.

Spooky Games for Halloween

When I was a child we always celebrated Halloween. We would hang up witches made from black sugar paper on fishing wire and hack out the insides of pumpkins. The night was also about trick or treating. I have vivid memories of walking the cold, late October streets with a gaggle of mates with flapping capes, white faces, wonky fangs and a plastic bag of our winnings – Mini Mars Bars, Chocolate Eclairs, Quality Street and Mint Imperials. There is nothing more frightening than knocking on a stranger's door and announcing with false brio – trick or treat! One year we knocked on the wrong door.

Mr Harrison worked in the Roman Museum, which stood opposite my primary school. He was a rather dishevelled man with a pot belly, bald head and expansive beard. His association with Roman Britain heightened our feeling that here was a man with links to a more barbaric age. We would watch him from the playground as he left the museum every day to buy his lunch in the nearby pub.

One Halloween, a group of us dared each other to knock on his door. It was an agonizing decision but surely this was what trick or treating was all about? His wife opened the door and curtly informed us, 'We don't do trick or treating here', before firmly closing it in our faces. But

where was Mr Harrison? Unimpressed, someone suggested we spray Silly String through their letter box. This was our 'trick', which we'd never had the courage to use before, apart from on ourselves. So we reopened the gate, crept along the short path to the door, opened the letter box and let rip with the Silly String. Seconds later came a primordial roar. The door was flung open and out rushed Mr Harrison. We fled with him in hot pursuit, bellowing obscenities as he hurtled after us. Leaving a trail of discarded sweets and layers of costume behind us, we turned up a narrow alley, dashed across a set of front lawns and collapsed through our back door.

I am not sure if we ever quite got over the shock of being chased by Mr Harrison. We would watch him from the playground with a new fascination and awe. He was a man willing to lose it and we respected him for that. Trick or treating had become an extreme sport.

For grown-ups Halloween poses different problems. Gangs of adults marching the streets armed with canisters of Silly String and demanding Mini Snickers is likely to end in police prosecution. So what to do? Arriving at parties in a costume is fun but it's slightly strange having the usual conversations about politics, the credit crunch and the weather dressed as the Bride of Frankenstein.

My advice is to bin all attempts at polite discourse and instead embrace the spirit of mad costumes with equally mad games.

A Devilish Wedding

This time of year has always had a spooky tinge. The Anglo-Saxon term for November was *Blod-monath* (Blood Month) as this was when surplus livestock was slaughtered to save on fodder and when other animals were offered as sacrifices. The origin of Halloween itself lies in the Irish ritual of *Samhain* (pronounced Sarwin), which fell on 1 November. This word meant 'summer's end' and the festival marked the beginning of the new year. In medieval Irish folklore the night before was always associated with fairies, ghosts and the supernatural. Traditionally, Halloween has always been observed most keenly in Celtic areas of the country, including Scotland, where the night included traditional dancing and children dressing up and visiting houses to collect pennies (a custom that would later become trick or treating).

The two games described below are good because they're both messy. They are about getting a face full of flour and splashing your fellow contestants with cold water. Playing them in costumes actually helps because these are games about making a fool of yourself and going for it. Played in the right way, they can help restore the lost exhilaration of Halloween.

Traditionally, these two games come as a pair; you wash the flour from your face in the water of the apple tubs.

Flour Cake

As many as you like

Seductively easy

Plate, pudding basin, large knife and a piece of chocolate

20 minutes

You need a smooth basin of around eighteen centimetres in diameter and ten centimetres in depth. Fill the basin with flour right to the brim and make sure it's quite compacted. Put a wooden chopping board on top, then invert it and leave for an hour or so to form its shape.

When everyone is assembled and ready to play, bring the board ceremoniously into the room and place it on a small, low table. Then gently lift the basin off the board, leaving a beautiful, smooth mound of flour. Finally, place a square of chocolate on the summit of the mound.

Take a large knife and, as you pass round in the circle, players approach the cake one by one. Each player must slice the cake. The aim is to prevent the cake from collapsing and the chocolate from falling with it.

People are always convinced that the cake will fall after just a few slices. But flour is much stronger than that. If everyone is reasonably careful and you are playing with, say, twenty people, you'll find that the mound will, amazingly, sustain a couple of slices per person. When the chocolate finally tumbles, the person who has made the final, fateful slice must put her arms behind her back and dive into the flour to rescue it with her teeth. At which point everyone pushes this unfortunate person's face further into the flour as she tries to retrieve the chocolate. The player should come up for air plastered with flour, at which point the tradition is that she stick her head into the water bucket for the apple bobbing; the water combines with the flour to make a glue-like paste which gives the player an unearthly white coating.

This person might never come back to your house again.

Apple Bobbing

No limit

Medium to surprisingly hard

Apples, washing-up bowls, buckets, chairs, towels

30 minutes

Apples have always been highly valued in Britain. In the Celtic age the penalty for cutting down an apple tree was death and in folklore the fairy islands lying to the west of England were said to be covered with apple orchards. Avalon, the island to which King Arthur was taken to heal his wounds after his last battle, means Isle of Apples. It's not surprising, then, that we have a host of rituals and games connected with apples.

One old tradition connected with this time of year was a custom which revealed the identity of the person you would marry. Young men and women would peel a long, unbroken strip of skin from an apple and then throw it over their left shoulder. From the shape the peel made when it landed on the ground, you could discover the initial of the man or woman you would marry. Another spooky example can be found in Robert Burns' poem 'Halloween', written in 1785. In the poem Jennie asks whether she might 'eat the apple at the glass', which her granny sternly forbids her to do. This is a reference to the belief that if a young woman eats an apple in front of a looking glass at Halloween the face of the man she is destined to marry will appear in the mirror, looking over her shoulder.

Divide the company into two equal-sized teams.

Take two normal washing-up bowls, fill them both with

water and place them on two separate chairs. Take as many apples as there are players and divide them equally between the bowls. Now make each team stand the same distance away from the bowls behind a starting line. Appoint two team captains and ask them to establish a running order by giving each member of their team a number. At the starting signal, both number ones race to the bowls and kneel with their hands behind their backs. They must lift an apple out of the water using only their teeth and drop it by the side of the bowl. After doing this, they must race back to their team and tag the next player who then runs up to the bowl. The first team to empty their bowl wins.

You have to strictly enforce the no hands' rule. But by all means encourage people to give their opponents a little shove by placing the two chairs close to each other. You want the pace to be fast and furious. Encourage cheering.

If all goes well and the company is hungry for more, you can move to the next level. The deeper the container the harder it is to get the apples out. So now you can bring out two builders' buckets and play the game all over again at the advanced stage. As the buckets contain more water you will need to have lots of newspaper and towels to soak up the overspill. You can advertise this round as being only for those brave enough to take part. It's absolutely riotous. For those worried about their frocks, there is plenty of opportunity for umpiring and cheerleading roles.

Flour Cake and Apple Bobbing are both physical, climactic games that go back centuries. Both have the potential to whip your guests into a frenzy. Although your guests may beg you for more, both games are notoriously hard to follow. My answer would be to encourage fun of a more freestyle kind: turn up the music, drink plenty of mulled wine and get dancing.

Christmas Games

Christmas is a hard time to get right. We are all faced with the challenge of trying to make a special day, of creating an occasion of rare intensity that lives up to all our expectations. Although there are traditions to help us – turkey, crackers, the Queen's speech – these can pretty quickly be exhausted. In fact, I would be quite happy if I never pulled another cracker again in my life. So the challenge is how to renew the power of Christmas? How to keep it fresh and genuinely fun?

Games have been part of Christmas ever since its beginnings in the midwinter holidays of the later Roman Empire. We know that from late November until the end of January there was a long list of festivals. The most important of these were the Saturnalia, which began on 17 December and ended on 24 December, the Birthday of the Unconquered Sun on 25 December and the Kalends, which began on 1 January.

These events were shot through with the spirit of celebration and playfulness. Buildings were decorated with evergreens, presents were given and men dressed up in women's clothing and animal skins. This was a time when normal roles were reversed and special licence was given to forbidden pleasures. Gambling with dice, normally forbidden, was allowed and a mock ruler presided over the festivities. A slave temporarily became the lord of his master. The classical poet Lucian, writing in the second century, described one such Saturnalia as defined by 'drinking, and being drunk, noise and games and dance, appointing of kings and feasting of slaves, singing naked, clapping of hands, occasional ducking of corked faces into icy waters'.

Now this sounds fun (especially the naked singing). However, the arrival of Christianity into Britain meant big changes. Naked singing was out. Hymn singing was in. The Church embarked on a campaign of taking over existing rituals and replacing them with events marking the Christian year. And this explains the conflict that lies at the heart of our experience of Christmas. What was once a celebration of misrule, liberty and excess had become, by the third century AD, a religious festival, a sacred, solemn event celebrating the virgin birth.

Traditions connected with the lord of misrule, however, continued to find expression. Throughout the medieval and Renaissance periods, Christmas was still known as a time when normal conventions were turned on their head. Twelfth Night became a crucial part of the celebration and it was on this night that a pea and a bean were baked in a cake, and those who found them were crowned king and queen for the night. It was during the nineteenth century, largely through the influence of Prince Albert and Charles Dickens, that Christmas developed a new focus on the family. Alongside Dickens' new myth of the perfect Christmas, Prince Albert introduced the Christmas tree, which became a symbol of the happy family gathering. People saw ways of cashing in on the emerging Christmas economy and so Christmas cards, crackers and commercially produced Christmas puddings all arrived on the scene.

But crazy games kept going. Snap Dragon was a popular game played on Christmas Eve. Brandy was poured over raisins and lit. The lights were put out and in the eerie darkness each person would have to snatch a raisin from the flames. As one Victorian commentator wrote, it was 'somewhat of an arduous feast, requiring both courage and rapidity of action; a considerable amount of laughter and merriment is evoked at the expense of the unsuccessful competitors'. I imagine trying to fish out flaming raisins was a fairly harrowing business and I dread to think what might have befallen the 'unsuccessful competitors'.

But I was intrigued to find out for myself. When I first attempted to bring back Snap Dragon my efforts ended badly. Having promised some friends the revival of a great Victorian tradition, I had gone to the supermarket and bought some snack-size boxes of raisins and sloshed some cheap brandy over them. I brought them to the table in a large bowl, turned off the lights and applied a lighted match. Nothing happened. Where were the enveloping flames? After several failed attempts, the lights went back on and I was left to chew forlornly on some damp raisins while the evening continued.

My curiosity in playing the game was only heightened and I got in touch with a friend called Martin who was a part-time chef and cookery writer. Why did my raisins not light? Martin explained that they had to be already hot. He pointed out that the Victorians would have had a range of chafing dishes, silver plates and spirit lamps to help them heat the mixture and keep it warm. So, with Martin's help, I put together a method/recipe for this long-lost game.

Snap Dragon

Unlimited

Advanced, you have to be bold (or maybe a little stupid)

Raisins, brandy, flameproof plate

Preparation & playing 20 minutes

Buy a small bottle of brandy with a high alcohol percentage, 40 rather than 36 per cent. This will help the liquid to burn. Pour around half of the bottle over three large handfuls of dried raisins and let the mixture steep for half an hour or so.

When you are ready to play, put the mixture into a small saucepan and warm gently. You don't want it to boil otherwise you will start burning off the alcohol. At the same time, warm up a large, flameproof plate. You can do this either by popping it into the microwave for thirty seconds or by resting it over a boiling saucepan of water for a couple of minutes. Then take the warmed mixture and pour it onto the plate. It's good to use a plate with a lip, the kind of thing you would carve a roast chicken on. Turn off all the lights and ignite the brandy.

The brandy will burn very quickly to begin with and I recommend that you don't start shoving your hand in at this stage. Wait for a minute or so and then very carefully try and pick out the raisins.

Watching the raisins burning in the brandy is extremely dramatic. The blue flames leap from one side of the plate to another, rising and falling; it's like watching an electric storm from above. With the flames at their height, approaching the raisins seems like an act of total madness. It is. However, as the flames begin to die down you will find that they will move around the plate and there will be seconds when a raisin is not flaming and then you can grab it.

For a few moments, just before the flames die out altogether, a sort of hysteria sets in with people abandoning caution and plucking out as many raisins as possible before the heat is completely extinguished. The raisins themselves are rather delicious – although avoid those that have become completely blackened. You will also have a lot of tepid brandy left over. I asked Martin the best thing to do with it. He suggested using it to make Spanish coffee ('the sort that old men drink in bars in the morning, which are often more brandy than coffee'), as a sauce for puddings ('especially ones where raisins and brandy are involved') or simply to make the losing player drink it. Now that sounds like a good idea.

Playing the game today, you become aware of its symbolic properties. In a time of darkness and piercing cold, here was an extravagant and spectacular game made for its season; a game full of the wonder and spectacle of Christmas.

In centuries past, for those who couldn't afford Snap Dragon there was always 'Flap Dragon'. This was a very old game which stretched back at least as far as Shakespeare. Falstaff refers to a character who 'drinks off candled ends for flapdragons'. In the game a player has to drain a mug of ale or cider, in the mouth of which is a lighted candle. This was not a game I wanted to try.

Another remnant of Christmas' wild origins has been preserved through the presence of mistletoe. Mistletoe was a plant used in ancient Celtic fertility rites and so predates even the Roman Saturnalia. It was traditionally excluded from churches because of its sexual associations but it began to enjoy a huge renaissance during the mid-nineteenth century. Indeed, in an age when a game of blind man's buff was your best chance of a festive frolic, you can see why mistletoe was such an exciting prospect. In December 1842 *Punch* picked up on this, describing legions of ravenous Victorian ladies looking to land an unsuspecting young gentleman: 'single ladies of five and thirty lay in large stocks of lip salve to prepare for the chances of the mistletoe bough'. The traumas of negotiating 'the bough' were brought home to the American author Nathaniel Hawthorne while staying in a boarding house in Southport in 1855. He describes the ravenous maidservants taking joyful advantage of the branches hanging from the gas fittings: 'it is very queer being so customarily so respectful that they should assume this license now, absolutely trying to pull the gentlemen into the kitchen by main force and kissing them the harder and more abundantly the more they were resisted'. Once again, we have a ritual which acts as an excuse for a contact that is normally forbidden. Perhaps the naked singing was not so far away, after all.

Telegrams

3 - 15

Advanced

Pen and paper

20 minutes

Telegrams were always a source of drama. The arrival of a telegram would signify an event of high importance – the birth of a child or the death of a loved one. They were expensive and so were used only when absolutely necessary. The challenge here is to convey high stakes while negotiating the game's crazy parameters.

Players are given pens and paper. One of them chooses a word. Everyone must now write a telegram as an acronym of this word. So, if the word is 'Christmas' then the first word must begin with C, the second with H and so on. In order to match the telegram style you need to write a sentence with an imperative feel about it – it must contain information in the form of an urgent message. The telegrams must also be related to the original word. The pleasure of this game lies in the amazing constructions people produce under this pressure. Notable examples that I have collected from recent Christmases include: Monkeys Undermining Scaffolding Evacuate Under Masonry (MUSEUM), Please Help I've Lost Overall Sense Of People's Happy Yearnings (PHILOSOPHY) and Behold

Angels Singing In Lofty Ivory Cornices Above for the advanced example of BASILICA.

Depending on your mood, people can just share their telegrams and you can celebrate the amazing examples they have come up with, or you can award points. If you want to score, I would recommend awarding three points to the top telegram, two to the second and one to the third. You will need to establish quality by consensus, but it's normally clear which ones are the best. At the end of four or five rounds declare a winner.

The Station Game

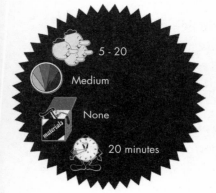

5 - 20

Medium

None

20 minutes

This is a good game to play after dinner and when there are lots of you. A good time is New Year's Eve, as this game can intrigue everyone, irrespective of age. You can also adapt its level of difficulty according to the age groups you are playing with.

Somebody starts by volunteering a train journey. He must give the starting station and the destination. This person must also establish a particular 'secret' in how he explains his journey.

For example, he might say, 'I travelled from Edinburgh to, um, London'. The next person must now give her journey. She might say, 'I travelled from Glasgow to Birmingham', to which the first player would reply, 'No, you didn't'. Why not? Because the second player hasn't yet recognized that the secret to this round is that you have to say 'um' between the first and second station.

The next few people would all offer their journeys, all being told 'No, you didn't' – until someone round the circle might, by accident, say 'um' between their stations. The reply would then come, 'Yes, you did'. Gradually the group will begin to figure out why certain journeys are allowed and others not. When the go falls again to the first player, he gives another example of a successful journey, once again repeating the clue, saying, for example, 'I went from Bristol to, um, Manchester'.

As people guess the code, they are able to make successful journeys and, hopefully, the secret will become clear to all. It's nice giving all the players time to guess the secret so that everyone can make at least one successful journey. The first person who cracks the code should be the one to establish a new code for the next round. Remember, the code can be built around how you say the journey or the content of the journey itself; for example, you might always travel to or from stations of one syllable or the destinations might always start with the same letter. There are infinite variations.

In the Manner of the Word

3 - 20

Easy

None

30 minutes

This game is about acting out gestures in the manner of a word, which one player has to guess. The game features in Noël Coward's play *Hay Fever*, which is all about the eccentric Bliss family. In this extract various characters try to explain the rules to newcomer Richard:

JUDITH: Choose an adverb, and then –

SIMON: Someone goes out, you see, and comes in, and you've chosen a word among yourselves, and she or he, whoever it is, asks you some sort of question, and you have to –

SOREL (moves up to Simon): Not an ordinary question, Simon; they have to ask them to do something in the manner of the word, and then –

SIMON: Then, you see, you act whatever it is –

SOREL: The answer to the question, you see?

RICHARD (apprehensively): What sort of thing is one expected to do?

JUDITH: Quite usual things, like reciting 'If', or playing the piano –

RICHARD: I can't play the piano.

SIMON: Never mind; you can fake it, as long as it conveys an idea of the word.

JACKIE: The word we've all thought of?

SOREL (impatient): Yes, the word we've chosen when whoever it is is out of the room.

And the chosen word is 'winsomely'.

One player leaves the room, while the others decide on an adverb: slowly, tenderly, seductively, violently, sadly, surprisingly, for example. This person is called back in and must ask the others to perform actions in the manner of the word that has been chosen. Simple actions are best to start with, such as smiling, pouring a glass of wine, eating a peanut or reciting a nursery rhyme. Actions involving other people are fun, too, like asking someone on a date or interviewing them for a job. The player who left the room can ask for as many activities as he needs until he has successfully guessed the adverb. When he does, someone else has a go.

Charades

6 - 20

Medium

Pens and paper for each team

1 hour

No book of games would be complete without a version of Charades. It's so famous that it's known simply as The Game. Charades began as a game of riddles. These were normally written in verse and known as Enigmas. There is a games manual from 1711 called Delights for the Ingenious, *which contains some examples:*

From the mate of the cock, winter corn in the ground
The Christian name of my friend may be found:
Join the song of a cat, to the place hermits dwell in,
Gives the surname of him who does music excel in.

Fortunately the book provides an explanation, too:

Here the mate of a cock is a **hen***: the winter corn is either wheat or ry; but because it is to make up a name, it is the latter that is meant; so the Christian name is* **Henry***. Then the song of a cat is what we call the pur of a cat; and the place a hermit dwells in is called a* **cell***; so the surname is* **Purcell***; so that this rebus is the name of M. Henry Purcell, the late famous Master of Music, perhaps the best that England ever bred.*

During the nineteenth century, Charades moved from being a word game to an acting game. On 12 November 1812, the novelist Maria Edgeworth, who was touring the country houses of England, wrote to her sister:

> We acted **words** – charades last night –
>
> **Pillion**. Excellent. First we entered swallowing pills with great choking – Pill – next on all fours roaring lions – Fanny and Harriet roaring devouring lions much clapped – Next as to my tout – Enter Bertha riding on Mr Smith's back **pillion**.

There is a tone of excitement here. I recognize it. It's the feeling you get when you play a really good game for the first time. This seems as close as possible to the beginnings of the game as we know it.

The games historian Tony Augarde is also a compiler of dictionaries and he has suggested that the word charade itself probably comes from the Portuguese charrado, meaning 'conversation', or the Spanish word charra, meaning 'chatter', but he also mentions the Spanish word charrada, meaning the 'speech or action of a clown'. I like the idea of charades being an amalgam of these meanings: the chattering of clowns.

Gradually, Charades became so popular that it began to develop its own language of gestures to illustrate the titles of films, plays, books and songs. Its presence in homes across the country led to it becoming known simply as The Game. And its nationwide popularity was guaranteed when it became an ITV game show: Give Us a Clue. I think

this is the one and only time a parlour game has achieved viewing figures in the millions.

You have two teams. Each writes down a list of titles: films, TV shows, books, plays, musicals, operas. The game begins with one team selecting a member of the opposing team. They are taken outside and told their title, which they then must act out to their own team. They are given two minutes to do so. If the team guesses the title correctly they are awarded a point and the game continues with each team being given a new title in turn until everyone has had a go. Difficult titles that have to be broken down word by word and syllable by syllable are the most fun. *Superman* can be guessed in seconds but *A Guide to British Theatre in the Twentieth Century* takes rather more effort. If the company is up for it, being ambitious brings great rewards.

Not everyone has proved a fan of the game. Maybe, for the sake of games dissenters everywhere, we should give the last words on The Game to Ogden Nash:

> I do not know its name.
> Mostly it's called The Game.
>
> Or sometimes Indications
> Or other variations.

But whatever be its name,
I was happy ere it came.

But now it has come,
I'm a bum.

Figure of fun and shame
I do not like The Game.

To be honest, to be candid,
I do not understand;

I amn't very good at it,
I'm never understood at it.

I am seized by mental gout
When acting phrases out.

I am lost in foggy mazes
When guessing others phrases.

I'm a gabbling babbling moron
At quotations from the Koran.

Yea, even Mother's Goose's
Leave me stammering excuses.

Be mine, be mine the blame,
But I do not like The Game ...

Many enjoy it vastly,
I find it ghastly.

New Year in Swiss Cottage

After university I lived in a small room in Willesden Green. A group of friends lived nearby, in three flats all next to each other, above a row of shops in Swiss Cottage. Everyone was trying to break into sketch comedy and fringe theatre. Whenever you went round there you would find people waiting for the phone to ring. Everyone was 'broke and bored'.

Games became a good way to kill time. The best time to visit was New Year. There were always loads of games as well as the infamous ritual of hot corks. This involved warming corks in the flame of a candle. When one end was soft you would apply the cork like lipstick to your face to draw moustaches, raised eyebrows, sideburns, goatees, even full beards. Everyone would parade around the room with elaborate facial hair and exaggerated beauty spots. These makeshift masks gave the evening a unique sense of freedom and bizarre hilarity.

Ibble Dibble

5 - 30

Easy

Candles, corks

15 minutes

Inspired by my fun with corks I did some hunting around and discovered this old naval game, which was apparently played on submarines by sailors with little else to do.

Everyone playing is a given a number, prefixed with the words Ibble Dibble. So people are Ibble Dibble One, Ibble Dibble Two, Ibble Dibble Three etc. On the table are one or two corks and a candle. Let's say I am Ibble Dibble One and the player opposite me is Ibble Dibble Two. I start by saying, 'Ibble Dibble One with no dibbles to Ibble Dibble Two with no dibbles'. Ibble Dibble Two then responds by naming another player, saying, 'Ibble Dibble Two with no dibbles to Ibble Dibble Three with no dibbles'. And so on until someone makes a mistake by saying the wrong words in the wrong order or by hesitating.

The player who has made the mistake is now branded on the face with a warm cork. He can brand himself or you can appoint a brander. He will now have a spot on his face and so now have 'one dibble'. So, if Ibble Dibble Two is branded, he will now be known as 'Ibble Dibble Two with one dibble', and he must begin the new round by saying, 'Ibble Dibble Two with one dibble to Ibble Dibble One with no dibbles'. And a new round commences, with each player referring to himself and the player he is addressing, until someone makes a mistake. Dibbles are the increasing number of marks on each player's face.

Children love this game because it's a chance to get a very dirty face. The idea is to get at least one player's face covered with ash by the end.

Eating Eggs at Easter

When I was growing up, Easter was entirely about whether to wish for the Twix, Snickers or Mars Easter egg. Or there was the option of a Jumbo Chocolate Orange instead. After an orgy of Easter chocolate consumption, I would store the remains in my bottom drawer alongside my V-neck school jumpers. It was too painful to part with any of the delectable chocolate. Once squirrelled away, the egg and its contents would be forgotten – only to be discovered by Mum some months later, having turned a strange, mottled white colour. It's only as I've grown older that I've discovered more about the noble games associated with Easter.

Shrove Tuesday used to be about more than just pancakes. This was the day of the annual village football match, something quite different from our experience of games and sports today. We are used to watching small numbers of players competing in a tightly defined space, but football grew out of a mass game played by hundreds. A great example of this was the annual match at Derby, which was played between the two parishes of St Peters and All Saints. The game was essentially open to everyone and people travelled from around the country to take part. Kick-off was at 2.00 p.m. on Shrove Tuesday in the marketplace. At the height of its popularity at the beginning of the nineteenth century, the game was attracting between five hundred and a thousand people on each side. The aim was to carry the ball about a mile out of town, with one side trying to reach the gate of a field on one side and another the wheel of a distant watermill. As you can imagine, cheating was hard to police. Players would hide the ball or remove its insides and transport it under their shirts. I suspect the game finally conked out when all the players were either too wet, drunk or confused to carry on.

Football in the shape that we know it now emerged from teams that congregated around local pubs. These teams began to organize tournaments and gradually a set of rules began to emerge. One example of a local pub team that made it big was Newton Heath, which was based at the Three Crowns on Oldham Road in Manchester. Some years later they changed their name to Manchester United. Everton began its life at the Queen's Head pub in Everton village and the link between pub and team carried on late into the nineteenth century. In 1894 three professional teams, Gainsborough Trinity, Nottingham Forest and Manchester City, were all still getting their kit on in their local pubs before walking to their grounds.

If the Shrove Tuesday football match has largely died out, our love affair with Easter eggs has not.

The egg is one of the most adaptable symbols in European myth and ritual. It is frequently connected with spring and can symbolize new life, birth and regeneration. In Christian symbolism the egg can represent Christ overcoming death or even the stone rolled away from the front of his tomb. Eggs were also traditionally banned during Lent, so it's not surprising that Easter Day includes a celebration of their return.

One traditional game that has remained alive today is the Preston Pace-Egg Rolling Event. Pace comes from the Old English word *Pasch*, meaning Easter, and the ritual takes place on Easter Monday in Preston. Here crowds of people roll brightly coloured Pace-eggs down a slope and the player whose egg rolls furthest wins.

In terms of smaller scale games, playing catch with a raw egg is good fun. You stand in a circle and throw the egg gently from person to person. There is always one nervous participant who makes an anxious lunge at the flying egg, clasping it a little too tightly, with disastrous consequences. Another traditional egg game is for two players to balance their eggs on a spoon and fight a duel. The aim is to be the first player to force your opponent's egg from his spoon without yours falling off first. You can also hide eggs in the garden and devise your own egg hunt with clues leading you from one place to another, with teams racing to find the prize egg containing the treasure. However, in my experience the weather is unreliable at this time of year and it's often too cold to enjoy being outside. So, as a result, I would like to share the art of blowing eggs with you. There is something very calm and relaxing about doing this which takes you straight back to primary school; you don't have to think about anything and you can just concentrate on making a lovely object. It's less of a game than an activity but it's still great fun.

Pace-Eggs

In his book *The English Year*, the folklorist Steve Roud traces the history of decorating eggs. The earliest mention we have comes from 1778, when William Hutchinson wrote in his *History of Northumberland*, 'the children have dyed and gilded eggs given to them, which are called "Paste Eggs"'. The practice of decorating eggs grew more and more popular during the nineteenth century. John Brand, in his *Observations on the Popular Antiquities of Great Britain* (1849), wrote this account, which gives a precious glimpse into an extraordinary and delicate process:

> In the North of England, it is still the custom to send reciprocal presents of eggs at Easter to the children of families respectively betwixt whom any intimacy exists. The eggs being immersed in hot water for a few moments, the end of a common tallow candle is made use of to inscribe the names of individuals, dates of particular events, etc. The warmth of the egg renders this a very easy process. Thus inscribed, the egg is placed in a pan of hot water, saturated with cochineal; the part over which the tallow has been passed is impervious to the operation of the dye; and consequently when the egg is removed from the pan, there appears no discoloration of the egg where the

inscription has been traced, but the egg presents a white inscription on a coloured ground. The colour of course depends upon the taste of the person who prepared the egg; but usually much variety of colour is made use of. Another method of ornamenting 'pace eggs' is, however, much neater although more laborious, than that with the tallow candle. The egg being dyed, it may be decorated in a very pretty manner, by means of a penknife, with which the dye may be scraped off, leaving the design white, on a coloured ground.

For the Victorians decorating eggs was a serious business and they used a wide variety of natural dyes such as onion skins and saffron. Late in the century, shops began to sell professionally decorated eggs and then, in 1875, John Cadbury launched the first commercial chocolate egg.

Easter was changed forever.

Blowing Eggs

Unlimited

Dependent on ambition

Eggs, needles, paints, brushes

About an hour

Take your egg and with a needle make a small hole in both ends. Now try and blow the yolk and white out of one end. If you don't manage it, no problem; just use the needle to increase the size of the hole. (Experienced blowers seem to be able to blow through the tiniest aperture, but to get this good takes time.)

When your egg is empty, rinse it very gently under the cold tap (warm or hot water will cause anything left in the shell to cook). You want to eliminate the chance of unwelcome aromas interfering with the long life of your new creation. Now you come to the painting stage. You might find it easier to stand the egg in an egg cup, or just hold it gently between your fingers, as you create a tapestry of miniature chicks, flowers and ribbons. Once you've finished you can hang your eggs in the window or collect them in a basket. Any really great ones you can keep to bring out the following year.

3
GAMES *of*
MURDER
and MAYHEM

Three Games of Murder and Mayhem

'It was true that he felt ill, a sick empty sensation in his stomach and a rapidly beating heart, but he knew that the cause was only fear, fear of the party, fear of being made to hide by himself in the dark' – Graham Greene, 'The End of the Party'

'The End of the Party' is a spooky and poignant short story about being frightened of the dark. Francis and Peter are twin brothers who have been invited to the annual party of Mrs Henne-Falcon. Francis begs his mother to be spared going. He is terrified that they will play Hide and Seek in the dark, like last year, when he screamed and had to be taken home early. But his appeal fails and he is escorted to the party with his brother. At the party after the 'egg and spoon races, three legged races, and the spearing of apples' the dreaded moment for Hide and Seek comes. The lights are extinguished and the brothers lose each other in the darkness. Peter, desperate to reassure his brother, discovers him hiding 'between the oak bookcase on the left of the study door and the leather settee'. But for

Francis the ordeal proves too much. In a terrible twist of fate it is Peter's arm, reaching out to reassure Francis in the dark, which proves too much for his brother's fragile heart. When the lights are restored, little Francis has died of fright.

In only a few pages Greene exposes all the fears parties and playing games can provoke; the terror of other children and the fear of being humiliated as well as our deeper anxieties about being abandoned and lost in the dark. The games that follow are about evoking this fear but relishing every second of it. They are about being alone in the dark and waiting for the murderer to strike. And, as we get older, the thrill of these games doesn't abate. It intensifies.

Murder in the Dark

7 - 20

Medium

Cards, hat

1 hour

The 'roaring twenties' brought a new taste for pleasure and excess. Writing about the arrival of 'Jazzmania', the Daily Mail *described a new world of* 'women dressed as men, men as women, youths in bathing drawers and kimonos. Matrons moving about lumpily and breathing hard. Bald, obese, perspiring men ... dim lights, drowsy odours and futurist drawings on the walls and ceiling.' In London the Bohemian set appeared, defined by Robert Graves, 'by their keenness to use implements for unconventional purposes – to spread butter with a cut throat razor, drink tea out of a brandy glass, or use a dish swab as a hair net'. These Bright Young Things ushered in a new age of fancy dress parties and wild stunts. The Daily Mail *in 1924 described the* birth of the urban treasure hunt: 'A new Society Game. Midnight chase in London.' Players would meet and be given a list of objects to find, before being sent off in cars to find them and to congregate in the early hours at Piccadilly Circus or Charing Cross.

But underneath this apparent drive towards fun and frivolity, games from this period tell a more nuanced story. During this decade, games like Russian Sledges and Human Sacrifice began to appear in collections. These games remind me of early versions of Big Brother. Players have to justify staying in the game. The least convincing are voted out, to be 'thrown to a pack of hungry wolves' or given up for 'human sacrifice'. Games have become darker and the group is no longer an innocent, unreflective unit but a volatile community to be charmed and assuaged.

It seems impossible to ignore the shadow of the First World War. The exact origins of Murder in the Dark are impossible to fix but what is clear is that it emerged during this period. Perhaps people needed to negotiate somehow the horrors they had witnessed. Games were a safe way of doing this. So it's no surprise that playing hide and seek in the dark became Murder in the Dark.

Games had grown up.

Murder in the Dark is now a classic. Lying, squeezed under a bed, knowing that one of your fellow players is creeping through the shadows searching for his prey, is absurdly exciting. Adrenaline is the currency of this game, with the stakes quickly becoming high for the murderer, detective and all the quivering victims.

Darkness is essential. Sadly I live in a top-floor flat on a main road above a halal butcher's, so achieving the requisite pitch of blackness is hard. You need somewhere with thick curtains and not too much street light pouring in. But it's a fallacy to think you need a country house to play in. More than one level is good but otherwise all you need is a creaking staircase, a gloomy landing and plenty of dusty corners.

The last time I played this my eldest brother got wedged into a laundry basket and had to be pulled out by the Detective. So judge spaces carefully.

Before you start, it's a good idea to ask everyone to remove their shoes. The Murderer will need to be able to move around the house silently to evade the crime scene.

Tear up some small bits of paper. On one draw a cross, on another a circle. The rest leave blank. Make sure you have the same number of pieces as people playing the game. Throw them all in a hat and then pass it around. Everyone pulls out a piece of paper, being careful not to reveal what is written on it. The player who finds himself with the circle is the Detective and must reveal himself to the company as such. Whoever draws the cross is the Murderer and must remain silent.

The Detective stays by himself as the lights are turned off. It's important to try and get the whole house as dark as possible as everyone scatters and hides. In the enveloping darkness the Murderer must choose his prey and whisper into his ear, 'You're dead!' This is one means of dispatch. There are others. Most recently, I have come to enjoy the Murderer having to grip his victim gently on the back of the neck. The variations are endless. The victim must let out a blood-curdling scream, which is the cue for the Detective to turn on the lights.

As soon as the scream is heard everyone must freeze except the Murderer, who is allowed to make his flight from the crime scene. The Detective checks everyone's position before bringing them back to be interrogated. This is not a bluffing game (these come later) so everyone must answer the Detective's questions truthfully, apart from the Murderer. The Detective must then charge someone with the crime. If they are right, the Murderer must acknowledge his guilt and roles are reallocated to play again. However, if the Detective chooses wrongly the lights are again extinguished and the murders continue. Depending on the size of your group, the number of guesses the Detective is allowed varies. For a group of between eight and ten I wouldn't recommend giving him more than two guesses over two rounds before the Murderer is declared triumphant.

You can go further by building up the characters involved. You can make the room where the Detective waits the 'Police Station' and you can give everyone playing an identity and a name. If you have a good torch to hand you can introduce an element whereby, instead of the lights going back on, the Detective must scour the house with his torch, establishing everyone's hiding place and position at the time of the murder. Only when everyone has been found are the lights put back on and the interrogations begun, in the relative safety of the 'Police Station'.

Live Cluedo

This is a game to play on holiday. If you are away for longer than a weekend, it's good to impose a time limit of a couple of days.

Part of the fun of this game is the preparation. As soon as you arrive you'll need to scout out the space carefully and then compose your clues. As soon as you've given them out there is an immediate frisson as suddenly everyone takes on the shape of a potential assassin.

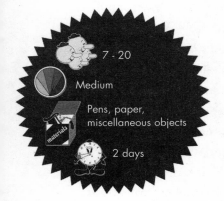

7 - 20

Medium

Pens, paper, miscellaneous objects

2 days

At the beginning of the game give all the players a piece of paper containing three pieces of information: who they must kill, their weapon and the location of the murder. When each guest has read their instructions, collect all the papers again, as they must be kept top secret. Players now have two days to find themselves alone with their target, with the murder weapon in hand and in the prescribed location.

When you are writing your instructions, make sure you choose objects and places that are not too difficult to achieve; 'with a can of beans outside the front door' or 'with a frying pan in the garden' are both good ones;

'with a dictionary in the pub' is not such a good one. You want to set people challenges that require ingenious solutions without actually being impossible. When the players find themselves with their victim they must explain how they intend to kill them with their object as there are rewards later for the most creative method. Over the weekend have occasional meetings at which you discover who is still alive and who has passed to the other side. The aim is to remain alive for as long as possible and to carry out your murder successfully.

As well as frenzied attempts to smuggle a hardback book to the bottom of the garden, conceal a cricket stump in the bathroom or to engineer a lonely encounter under the washing line, one major pleasure of the game lies in the final information sharing. Be clear about the deadline: for example, eight o'clock on Sunday evening. When this moment arrives gather all the players in one room and ask people finally to reveal whether they are alive or dead.

Then ask people to share their attempts, successful or otherwise, to kill their victims or to elude capture. There will be some amazing accounts of the secret history underpinning the last few days – lucky escapes, botched killings and elegant solutions involving the most unlikely murder weapons. At this point you can reward the living with a glass of wine (or champagne, if you're feeling really flush) and present a small prize to the player who has come up with the wittiest means of using their object to dispatch their prey.

If you are playing with a group who have either played this game before, or who just seem especially confident, you can try this nice variation. Instead of revealing the object to their victims, in this version the murderers must devise a way for the victims to voluntarily grasp their own murder weapon. So in the specified location you might ask someone to 'pass me that spade', or 'hold this cereal box' or 'catch this tennis ball'. This is very much the advanced version, so only try it with a team of experienced mercenaries.

Werewolf

9 - 20

Advanced

Pens and paper, hat

1 hour

People are obsessed with this game. Alongside the Hat Game, Werewolf has the power to enter your life forever. One friend told me that he had even managed to introduce it to a party of Hollywood celebrities, who couldn't stop playing it. As the game is complicated I want to spend some time giving you a comprehensive description. It's worth the effort as this is a king among games.

There are various names for this game, including Mafia and Palermo. The game was invented in Moscow in the sixties by a Russian psychology student called David Davidoff. This makes sense as, at the heart of the game, is a study of how the mind works, what makes people good liars and who cracks under pressure.

The game is a contest between a community of citizens who must defend their town against a tribe of bloodthirsty murderers. I have played the game in its various manifestations and believe the one outlined below is the best. It's addictive and, like the very best games, grows in the playing. To acquire the right understanding of the strategies available, you need to play it over and over again. The central question the game poses is: can you lie convincingly?

Not least because I work in theatre, I enjoy the game most when it embraces characters and an imaginary world. Doing this also helps to lift the game out of the personal. It's a stressful game and people can *become upset. It's also unjust – innocent people will 'die'. So the more distance you have between yourself and the game the more playful and enjoyable it will become. Played in such a spirit, the game can become a rich journey into the shared fantasy of a group.*

This game needs a strong leader. When you are introducing the game to friends, make sure you have read these instructions carefully and that you've gone through them a few times in your head. Once you've played the game a couple of times, the rules will become second nature. The Leader begins by suggesting a world. This can be any standard community that those playing might enjoy being part of. I am going to use the example of a medieval village in Eastern Europe, but more possibilities are given at the end of these instructions.

Set the scene by explaining that this village is in the power of Werewolves. Every night they are killing innocent villagers. And their power is spreading. You are going to begin by giving people roles in this community, including assigning who the Werewolves are going to be.

At this stage, ask people to close their eyes before putting a folded-up piece of paper in each of their hands. You will have prepared these papers earlier on and here's how.

For between six and nine players you're going to need two Werewolves. For between ten and fifteen players you'll need three, and for sixteen players and above you'll need four. In this case let's assume you are playing with nine people, so mark two papers with a 'W' for Werewolf. There are two other special roles, that of the Doctor and that of the Seer, which I will explain later. For now, alongside the Werewolf papers, mark one paper with a 'D' for Doctor, another with an 'S' for Seer, and on the five remaining papers write 'V' for Villager.

Fold the papers up tightly and place them in a hat. Ask everyone to close their eyes. Now go round putting a piece of paper in each person's hand. When you've done this people should open their eyes, read what is written on their pieces of paper, fold them up again and replace them in the hat.

You will play the Town Mayor. For reasons that will become apparent later, the Doctor and Seer should not reveal themselves yet. And the Werewolves must disguise themselves at all costs. So, assume that everyone is a Villager and set the scene by asking everyone to choose a character from this sleepy village. People should choose an appropriate profession – blacksmith, tavern keeper, swine herd, village idiot (you know the sort of thing) – and make sure everyone comes up with a fictional name for themselves.

The game takes place over a series of 'days' and 'nights'. During the days, the Villagers meet and decide who they suspect of being a Werewolf. This person is then 'killed' with a silver bullet. During the night the Werewolves make their killing.

The game begins with the Villagers coming together for a town meeting to discuss their plight. At the beginning of this meeting, the Town Mayor asks everyone to go round and announce their names and professions. People should be encouraged to find a voice and physical likeness that match their character. After these introductions, the townsfolk must debate among themselves who appears to be the least convincing. During the first 'day', the Villagers haven't much to go on but they must establish who they believe is a Werewolf. After initial introductions, the Villagers must establish two 'suspects', both of whom must make a speech in their own defence, arguing why they are innocent. The company then votes on who should be killed.

The condemned may say their last words before being 'shot with a silver bullet' and leaving the game. The first 'death' is always an awkward moment. People can become upset when they are eliminated at such an early stage in the game. You should reassure this person that being out at this stage is not serious – he or she will have the pleasure of watching the rest of the game unfold. As the Mayor, you need to supervise this business carefully, bringing the Villagers to order if necessary.

Night comes and you ask everyone to close their eyes. When everyone's eyes are tightly shut, ask the true Werewolves to open their eyes. By pointing at someone the Werewolves agree which Villager they would like to kill. They then close their eyes.

Now ask the Doctor to open his eyes. The Doctor has the power to save someone, although never himself. The Doctor points at the person he wishes to save. If this person is also the Werewolves' victim then there are no killings that night.

Finally, the Seer only is asked to open his eyes. In the story the Seer is a character who has 'second sight'. The Seer may point to anyone in the circle. As the Mayor, you will reveal whether this person is a Werewolf or not. The Seer can choose to share this knowledge or not the following day.

Day breaks and everyone opens their eyes. The Mayor announces whether there has been a killing and who it was that has been slaughtered in the night. The Villagers then hold another meeting where they establish two more suspects, who both make speeches and one of whom is executed. Night falls and the process is repeated. The game continues moving from day to night until either all the Werewolves have been killed or all the Villagers wiped out.

As you play this game more and more often you'll get to know the strategies. Only the Mayor has objective knowledge. As people die, they take their secrets to the grave and must remain silent until the game's end. This means that anyone can claim to be the Seer or the Doctor, and often those who lie most audaciously win. The Mayor must also keep an eye on the clock and ensure that the days don't last too long and that the Villagers make their decisions with alacrity.

The thrill of this game lies in creating a rich world together. The Mayor needs to create a vivid picture of a world in turmoil and should provide gory details of each death as it is announced. As the Mayor, it's your job to maintain the drama and suspense. You are both umpire and storyteller.

The Villagers need to work together to defeat the Werewolves and they have to be ruthless and canny. The Werewolves need to be impeccable liars and find ways of winning the trust of the Villagers so as to allow their number to remain intact and their reign of terror to triumph.

Some things to remember:

If you are the Mayor always to refer the Werewolves in the plural, so as not to give away whether any have been killed or not.

Make sure when you are addressing the Werewolves not to move your head to address them directly. Keep speaking towards the centre of the room. The Villagers will be listening out for any kind of clues about who the Werewolves are and where they are sitting.

If you are a Werewolf make sure you are silent and as motionless as possible when deciding on your prey. Even the slightest movement or sound could give you away.

It's fun to make up new worlds every time you play. Players will have lots of suggestions but scenarios that I have discovered work especially well are:

Fifties America
English Village c. 1950
1930s Chicago
Yorkshire Dales
A Sicilian Village

If you go for an Italian setting then, of course, Werewolves can become Mafia. In other settings Vampires work well. Creatures with a human form but a monstrous underside that emerges only at night tend to work best.

Going Home Bag

What Makes a Good Games Master?

Playing games is an unreliable science. Unlike cookery, where it's just you, the food and an oven, playing games involves the most unpredictable element of all – other people. Other people can be notoriously difficult, moody, aggressive and reluctant to do anything new. So leading games is never easy and needs a balance of strength of personality, tact and good humour. When you get it right, people will be profoundly grateful. Most of us find social gatherings nerve-racking. Secretly, people want to be led and shown how to have a good time. So, as a games player, you are going to be a trailblazer. In order to assist you in your drive to make all your friends signatories to the great games revolution, here are seven top tips.

Prepare

If you are having a games party you will need to have seven or eight games up your sleeve. Even if you don't end up playing them all, you might be surprised at how many games people get through and you always want to have room to make last-minute changes, altering and swapping games as it becomes clearer which games are going down best. Also organize any papers and pencils etc before people arrive, so that one game can move smoothly into another.

Deal Well With People Who Are Out

If you are playing games with a large number of people (fifteen or over) avoid playing too many games where people go out. In big groups people quickly become restless and can try to disrupt others' concentration. If this happens, create a different space where people can go and commiserate with each other rather than hanging round being pests. I often assign a 'Kitchen of Shame' where people can go to get drinks or, when dealing with smaller numbers, a 'Sofa of Shame', where people must go and sit. By defining a space in this way you can keep people within the parameters of the game rather than leaving them feeling excluded.

Know When to Stop

I often get carried away and play too many games during the course of an evening. Fundamentally, games are a means to an end. Your aim is for people to have a good time so that they can feel more at ease with themselves and the other guests. Games also require work from your players. So leave plenty of time for breaks and for people to enjoy the benefits that game playing brings.

Hold On Tightly, Let Go Lightly

Crowds are unpredictable beasts so be prepared constantly to reshuffle your hand. You may have been convinced before people arrived that this would be the perfect night to play Murder in the Dark, but if the atmosphere isn't right be prepared to change your mind. You might find that Chinese Pictures or the Hat Game are a much better fit, or vice versa!

Have Something to Make Noise With

In his book *Endless Mirth*, the Victorian Charles Gilbert writes that the leader of a games evening might 'don a scarf or toga, or might carry a wand'. This would be fun but weird. What is useful is to have some kind of instrument to keep everyone's attention and to get games started. I use an old bicycle horn, but hitting a saucepan with a wooden spoon works equally as well.

Play to Win ...

As the games master you have to persuade everyone that your games are worth playing. To do this you have to approach them seriously and you have to play to win. If you don't care about the outcome no one else will.

... But It's Only a Game

As well as being prepared, focused and competitive you also need to be playful. Games can generate the most enormous rows, with people disputing the rules, sulking

when they are out or feeling paranoid they are being victimized. The list is endless. One Christmas recently I prepared a family quiz for Boxing Day, and nearly exploded with rage and grief when people didn't seem to be taking it seriously. These kinds of experiences teach us that being too precious doesn't help anyone.

Fundamentally, the greatest thing about games is that they don't matter at all. If everything goes pear-shaped, so what? Good for you for trying something different.

Epilogue

In the monastery library of San Lorenzo de El Escorial, a few miles outside Madrid, is a manuscript dating from 1238. It is ninety-eight pages long and bound in sheepskin. The *Libro de Juegos* – The Book of Games – is divided into four sections; the first part deals with chess, the second with dice games, the third with varieties of backgammon, and the fourth is a miscellany of games ranging from Grande Acedrez – an enlarged version of chess – to Alquerque, a simplified version of checkers. The book was the dream of King Alfonso X, King of León and Castile. By the time this book came to be written, he had supervised works on history, law, religion, astronomy and magic. Now he wanted a book of games.

The Book of Games was written in Spanish rather than Latin and is one of the first masterpieces in the European canon to be written in a colloquial language. Writing the book in Spanish rather than Latin was a choice. The king wanted his people to read and understand his book; he wanted them to play games. In his Introduction he wrote that his book was 'for those who like to enjoy themselves in private, avoiding the annoyance and unpleasantness of public places, or for those who have fallen into another's power, either in prison, or slavery, or as seafarers, and in general all those who are looking for a pleasant pastime, which will bring them comfort and dispel their boredom. For that reason, I, Don Alfonso, have commanded this book to be written.'

King Alfonso was the first collector of games. He realized it was important to gather examples of games so that they would never be forgotten. He understood that alongside the law, economics and religion, games were vital for the health of his citizens. But there is another, very different approach to games playing that I would like to end this book by sharing with you.

Let's fast-forward seven hundred years from that ancient manuscript to a black and white photograph taken in a French garden in 1907. Two middle-aged men are sitting astride a log. The log spans a makeshift swimming pool built into the ground using roughly hewn bricks. Both men are holding pillows. One of them, a large, burly figure with braces and a handlebar moustache, has one arm raised in the air, his pillow suspended mid-swipe. The other man is lifting his hand to defend his face. The photograph has the feeling of late summer, maybe even early autumn; the leaves look heavy on the trees. Almost out of shot, standing at one edge of the pool, is a woman dressed entirely in white. She is laughing.

This photograph was taken by the thirteen-year-old Jacques Henri Lartigue. Lartigue began taking photographs at the age of six and this photo is just one of a series he took of his family and friends playing an extraordinary array of home-made games, including building rafts, sailing down streams in oversized barrels, racing soap boxes on wheels and creating eccentric flying machines.

When I look at the photograph of these men on the log, I am entranced by the way this thirteen-year-old has captured two adults engaged with complete seriousness in a magnificently silly event. How did the duel come about? Was this the first pillow fight on the log, or was it a regular competition? Did the burly guy always win, or was the younger man fitter and faster? Was this about settling a grudge or winning a bet, or was it just that, on an afternoon in late summer, two men and a woman strolled into the garden to play a game?

King Alfonso's book and Lartigue's photograph represent two ends of the games spectrum. At one end we have the Spanish king's desire to compile and preserve a detailed account of all the games he knew. At the other is Lartigue's memento of two adults spontaneously having fun. Perhaps we need these two opposites that the monarch and the child represent. We need to remember the rules, while being inspired to create our own games whenever and wherever we please.

Playing and writing about the games in this book has brought it home to me that there is a part of us that never grows up. It might become harder to find it as we grow older, but there exists in all of us a memory of playing. When this memory is reawakened we can become happy to fish apples from buckets, discover hiding places in the dark, run blindfold around the house and play catch by the sea. We remember to live our lives like a game.

Acknowledgements

Tony Augarde's *The Oxford Guide to Word Games* was a precious store of ideas, information and references, for which I am very grateful. Thanks to Catherine Howells at the Museum of Childhood for making me feel so welcome and to Judith Flanders for making me feel like a writer. Thanks also to the brilliant Sophie, Charlotte and Kirsty at DGA and to Nick and Mark at Fourth Estate for their trust and enthusiasm. Special thanks to Lucy Barber, Tom Guard, Beatrice Hodgkin and Stephen Brown.

I couldn't have written this book without all the people who so kindly shared their games with me. Your generosity has made this book happen. I am especially indebted to a band of devoted players – Sebastian, Hugo, Harriet, Tessa, Olivia, Michael, Daniel and Emma – who spent many Sundays testing and refining the games in this book with unflagging gusto.

And the biggest thank you of all to Lootie.

Bibliography

Ackroyd, Peter, *Dickens* (London: Sinclair-Stevenson, 1990)

Augarde, Tony, *The Oxford Guide to Word Games* (London: Guild Publishing, 1984)

Bell, R. C., *The Board Game Book* (Los Angeles: The Knapp Press, 1979)

Brewster, P. G., *American Non Singing Games* (Norman: University of Oklahoma Press, 1953)

Briggs, Asa, *Victorian Cities* (London: Odhams Press, 1963)

Brimley Johnson, R., ed., *Selected Letters of Hannah More* (London: Bodley Head, 1925)

Caillois, Roger, *Man, Play and Games*, trans. Meyer Barash (London: Thames & Hudson, 1962)

Cohen, Morton N., ed., *Lewis Carroll: Letters* (London: Macmillan, 1979)

—, *Lewis Carroll: A Biography* (London: Macmillan, 1995)

Colvin, Christina, ed., *Maria Edgeworth: Letters from England 1813–1844* (Oxford: Clarendon Press, 1971)

Coward, Noël, *Collected Plays* (London: Methuen, 1999)

Cram, David, Jeffrey L. Forgeng and Dorothy Johnston, eds, *Francis Willughby's Book of Games: A Seventeenth-Century Treatise on Sports, Games and Pastimes* (Aldershot: Ashgate, 2003)

Crouch, Nathaniel, *Delights for the Ingenious* (London: Edmund Parker, 1732)

d'Astier, Martine, Quentin Bajac and Alain Sayag, eds, *Lartigue: Album of a Century* (London: Thames & Hudson, 2004)

Dickens, Charles, *A Christmas Carol* (London: Victor Gollancz, 1983)

Douglas, Norman, *London Street Games* (London: Chatto & Windus, 1931)

Flanders, Dorothy, *The Victorian House* (London: Harper Perennial, 2004)

—, *Consuming Passions: Leisure and Pleasure in Victorian Britain* (London: Harper Perennial, 2007)

Gilbert, Charles, *Endless Mirth* (London, 1874)

Gomme, Alice Bertha, *Traditional Games of England, Scotland and Ireland* (1898)

Graves, Robert, and Alan Hodge, *The Long Week-End: A Social History of Great Britain 1918–1939* (London: Faber & Faber, 1940)

Grunfeld, Frederick V., *Games of the World* (New York: Holt, Rinehart & Winston, 1975)

Herford, C. H., and Percy and Evelyn Simpson, eds, *Ben Jonson*, vol. 3 (Oxford: Clarendon Press, 1986)

Huizinga, J, *Homo Ludens* (London: Routledge and Kegan Paul, 1949)

Lancelyn Green, R., ed., *The Diaries of Lewis Carroll* (London: Cassell, 1954)

Logan, Thad, *The Victorian Parlour* (Cambridge: Cambridge University Press, 2001)

Mendel, Vera, Francis Meynell and John Goss, eds, *The Week-End Book* (London: Nonesuch Press, 1924)

Milne, A. A., *Not That It Matters* (London: Methuen, 1921)

Nash, Ogden, *Good Intentions* (London: Little, Brown and Company, 1942)

Opie, Iona, *Christmas Party Games* (New York: Oxford University Press, 1957)

Opie, Peter and Iona, *Children's Games in Street and Playground* (Oxford: Oxford University Press, 1969)

—, *Children's Games with Things* (Oxford: Oxford University Press, 1997)

Pepys, Samuel, *The Diary of Samuel Pepys,* ed. Henry B. Wheatley (London: George Bell and Sons, 1894)

Pick, J. B., *The Phoenix Dictionary of Games* (London: Phoenix House, 1952)

Pimlott, J. A. R., *Recreations* (London: Studio Vista, 1968)

—, *The Englishman's Christmas: A Social History* (Hassocks: Harvester Press, 1978)

Reid, Douglas A., *Playing and Praying: The Cambridge Urban History*, vol. 3, ed. Martin Daunton (Cambridge: Cambridge University Press, 2001)

Roud, Steve, *The English Year: A Month-by-Month Guide to the Nation's Customs and Festivals, from May Day to Mischief Night* (London: Penguin, 2006)

Scully, Frank, *Fun in Bed – The Convalescent's Handbook* (London: Heinemann, 1934)

Simpson, Jacqueline, and Steve Roud, *A Dictionary of English Folklore* (Oxford: Oxford University Press, 2000)

Strutt, Joseph, *The Sports and Pastimes of the People of England* (London: William Tegg, 1867)

Thurber, James, *Vintage Thurber*, vol. 1, with an introduction by Helen Thurber (London: Hamish Hamilton, 1963)

Tomalin, Claire, *Samuel Pepys: The Unequalled Self* (London: Viking, 2002)